The City of Everett dedicates this book to the people of Everett whose spirit, commitment, and ideals have shaped the community during its first century.

Mayor William ''Bill'' E. Moore

Everett City Council

Connie Niva, President
Bill Langus, Vice-President
Ed Diamond
Carl Gipson
Ed Morrow
Dale Pope
Bob Overstreet

Everett Park Board

Arlene Diamond, Chairperson
Ross Hoagland, Vice Chairperson
Gordon Hall
Don Hopkins
Dave Deveney
Dr. Don Barbacovi
Dr. Arthur Grossman

Robert C. Cooper, Director
Everett Parks and Recreation

THE
DONNING COMPANY
PUBLISHERS
NORFOLK/VIRGINIA BEACH

The History of
Everett Parks
A Century of Service and Vision

by Allan May and Dale Preboski

The Donning Company/Publishers
5659 Virginia Beach Boulevard,
Norfolk, Virginia 23502

Jim Shields, Managing Editor;
Susan Francisco, Managing Editor;
and Deborah Sager, Copy Editor,
for the City of Everett.

Edited at Donning by Elizabeth B. Bobbitt, Associate Editor, and Richard A. Horwege, Senior Editor

Library of Congress Cataloging-in-Publication Data:

May, Allan.
   The history of Everett Parks : a century of service and vision / Allan May and Dale Preboski.
      p.   cm.
   ISBN 0-89865-794-6
   1. Parks—Washington (State)—Everett—History—Pictorial works. 2. Parks—Washington (State)—Everett—History. 3. Everett (Wash.)—History—Pictorial works. 4. Everett (Wash.)—History. 5. Everett (Wash.)—Description—Views. I. Preboski, Dale, 1947-   . II. Title.
F899.E9M39   1989
979.7′71—dc20   89-27642
                                                     CIP

Contents

A Message From the Mayor

The face of Everett has changed from its early days. Once relying economically on mills, foundries, and refineries, Everett of the 1990s is a high technology center home to the Boeing Company, John Fluke, ELDEC, Honeywell, and Kohkoku. The once soley industrial Port of Everett has also become a popular recreational site as well with the second largest marina on the West Coast.

Located in the heart of the Pacific North-west, Everett is flanked by the Cascade Mountain Range, Port Gardner Bay, and the Olympic Mountains with the Snohomish River snaking through the north end of the city. Our past is still very much present in stately homes that overlook a picturesque waterfront.

A modern twentieth-century town, Everett offers some of the Northwest's greatest recreational opportunities. Swimming, tennis, golf, fishing, sailing, rowing and boating, kayaking and canoeing are just a few of the many activities available for recreation and leisure.

From its early beginnings to its present, the pioneers and industrialists of Everett have always had the vision to set aside park land for its citizens. As we near our 100th birthday, it is fitting that we pay tribute to those whose vision and foresight have created the beautiful and natural parks of our city. As Everett moves into the next century, we must continue to place an emphasis on expanding and maintaining our model park system. As our population continues to grow, our parks become increasingly more important for the health and welfare of our citizens.

We are proud to have some of the most beautiful parks in the state providing unique recreational opportunities for our children and our grandchildren. This book is dedicated to all those in our history who have donated their properties, personal time, resources, and talents toward developing this legacy.

I would like to extend a special thank you to Park Director, Bob Cooper, and his staff; Ralph Mackey who performed many hours of research; Dale Preboski and Allan May for organizing the research material into book form and to the many individuals and organizations who contributed to the success of this project.

Bill Moore
Mayor of Everett

Introduction

As Everett nears its one hundredth birthday and history becomes a popular topic of discussion, people are recalling that this city has a rich and fascinating past. Thanks to the direction of Mayor Bill Moore and the support of the City Council members, an important part of the city's past has been documented—the evolution of Everett's Park system. The history that is before you was published with the hope of capturing the people and events that helped create today's park system and prepare the foundation for the future.

This book is for the enjoyment of all residents and visitors of Everett. Everett's parks have, and will continue to play an important role in the lives of our citizens. By looking at the past, we will foster a renewed vision for the future of Everett.

**Robert C. Cooper, Director
Everett Parks and Recreation
Department**

Acknowledgments

As the City of Everett approaches its Centennial in 1993 it seems most appropriate that we reflect upon our past. It was with rare privilege that we had the opportunity to compile a history of Everett's park system.

The Parks and Recreation Department is indebted to many people who have assisted in the research, writing, editing, photography, coordination, and publishing of this book.

We would like to thank Mayor Bill Moore; Chief Administrative Assistant Pat McClain, and Mayor's Assistant Judy Davidson, whose vision and counsel brought the concept of a park history book to the City Council. We wish to thank the Everett City Council for approval of this project and for their continued support: Council President, Connie Niva, Vice-President, Bill Langus, Ed Diamond, Carl Gipson, Ed Morrow, Dale Pope, and Bob Overstreet.

The Everett Park Board deserves special thanks for their support and help in guiding this book through its formation and completion: Chairperson, Arlene Diamond, Vice-Chairperson, Ross Hoagland, Gordon Hall, Don Hopkins, Dr. Don Barbacovi, Dave Deveney, and Dr. Arthur Grossman.

The beginning of this book came about with the special research conducted by Ralph Mackey in 1987 and 1988. Ralph's dedication and contribution of personal time to this project has been invaluable and reflective of the commitment he has extended to the Park Department as a former Park Board member and Chairperson.

A very special thank you to Allan May and Dale Preboski. We were very fortunate to have the skill of these two very talented writers. Both spent many hours in reviewing the research and staff information and writing a book that we are extremely proud to have represent the Everett Parks Department.

Thank you to Deborah Sager for the many hours she spent editing this book. Her efforts brought a continuity of style to the writings of Allan and Dale.

The following organizations and businesses should be recognized for their contributions: Weyerhaeuser Paper Company, President, John H. Warchter; Scott Paper Company, President, Tom Fahey; the Everett Herald, Publisher, Larry Hanson; EVCC, President, Bob Drewell; the Snohomish County Museum, and the Minnesota Historical Society.

A number of individuals generously loaned photographs from their private collections and provided additional material and information: Mrs. Helen Jackson, Bob Humphrey, Bob Long, Sr., Bill Rucker, Nina O'Neil, Phyllis Royce, Mary Winspear, Ken Knudson, Jim Leo, Mike Dunn, Steve Burr, Elizabeth Moody Campbell, Doyle Cates, Mike Eason, Tom Gaskin, Will Sears, Mike VanWinkle, Jill Neff, and Mildred Neff.

Without help from the Everett Public Library, Director, Mark Nesse, this book would not have been possible. Particularly helpful were Margaret Riddle and Dave Dilgard, of the Northwest Room, who extended hundreds of hours working with park staff providing research information, photographs, and expertise to the project.

The following City departments provided helpful information: Everett Community Development Services, Director, Paul Roberts; Everett Planning Department, Director, Dennis Derickson; Everett Museum, Director, Brad Linder; Public Works Department, Director, Al Theal; Everett Police Department, Chief Al Shelstad; Fire Department, Chief Doug McNall; City Legal Office, Bruce Jones.

Thank you to former Chief Administrative

Assistant (to Bill Moore), Jim Langus. As my supervisor, Jim assisted me in putting together the necessary information for the Mayor and the City Council. His support and effort was invaluable to me both professionally and personally.

Recognition is due to all Park Staff including Superintendents, Harold Shaw, Hank Bowman, Ray Eubanks, and Administative Secretary Betty Ronning. Special thank you's to Kristie Guy and Kathleen Davis, for their assistance in typing the research work, photo captions, and miscellaneous articles; and also to Elizabeth Sutliff who spent countless hours at the copy machine. Special thanks to the Graphics and Marketing Division: Media Specialist, Mark Somers; Louis Fliger, photographer; Wayne Kilburn, graphic artist; Chris Hudyma, writer; Resource Coordinator, Jan Dorbolo; Duane Kirby Jenson, photo editor, for their invaluable assistance.

Lastly, I would like to thank Marketing Coordinator Susan Francisco, and Assistant Director Jim Shields, who coordinated the project. Their creativity and leadership brought this project from its earliest beginnings to a final product we can all be proud to have represent the Parks Department.

It has been my pleasure to work with all the individuals, organizations, businesses and city departments in Everett who have contributed to make this book a reality.

Robert C. Cooper, Director
Everett Parks and Recreation Department

Everett in the 1890s was in the height of a depression. Still citizens voted 613 to 26 in favor of a $30,000 park bond issue.
Everett Public Library

Chapter 1

The Early Years

Clark Park
Forest Park
Grand Avenue Park

Clark Park

Everett in 1892 was an infant city, but a booming one. Henry Hewitt and his partners in the Everett Land Company had seen their dream become reality and would see it crash in the depression of 1893. It was hardly the time to establish the city's first park, but somehow, it happened just that way.

The city's first three years saw Hewitt's group building a barge works, a nail factory, a paper mill, a shipyard, a street railroad, and a waterworks. A mineral deposit in the Monte Cristo district deep in the Cascade Mountains was under development, along with a smelter in Everett to process the ore. The $2 million Everett and Monte Cristo Railroad was being built to carry the ore. The development attracted many people, including John J. Clark, who left Wisconsin in 1892 and moved to Everett to invest $100,000 in one of the city's first commercial buildings.

The depression that began the next year halted the city's growth, and in many cases reversed it. By August, the Everett Land Company was in deep trouble.

About nine hundred laborers had jobs, but for eight hundred others in manufacturing wages had been cut 60 percent. About seven hundred were unemployed. The city's budget was $60,000, but its revenues were only $30,000,

The Clark Park Stumphouse was one of the symbols that represented Washington State in the St. Louis World Fair in 1902. The fir stump measured eleven feet and six inches in diameter.
Edson, photographer

and it cut expenses by turning out street lights and laying off most of its police officers. In 1893 the Everett Land Company offered to sell to the city its waterworks, electric works, and street railroad. A bond issue to finance the purchase was put to the voters in the spring of 1894 and failed.

But if the depression had left the people of Everett unwilling to tax themselves to buy streetcars, it had not dampened their desire for the finer things.

On January 9, 1894, at the height of the depression, Mayor Norton D. Walling called on the city council to buy land for parks: "One of the most influential and profitable educators among civilized nations, is the elevating influence of public parks and grounds," he said. In July, soon after the utilities bonds were defeated, the people of Everett voted 613 to 26 in favor of a $30,000 park bond issue. The city purchased

the block from Twenty-fourth to Twenty-fifth streets between Oakes Avenue and Lombard Street for $21,535 on September 27. Everett was in the park business. The new park was north of town and apparently saw little development during its earliest years, when it was called City Park.

By 1915, the park had a few facilities and a caretaker, and was being used for picnics and for church services. It became a meeting place for the community, complete with music on Sundays. In November 1919, the city marked $20,000 for a bandstand and other improvements. It was April 1921 before a bid was accepted from architect B. F. Turnbull. The town's musicians didn't wait for the bandstand. In July 1920, the Everett Municipal Band announced a series of concerts in the park. The first program included marches, music from several operas, and waltzes.

That concert began a long tradition of music and entertainment in the park that continued into the 1960s.

The park during the early days also was a center for public protests and meetings. In 1914, the timber mills in the city shut down for a week, locking out their employees in a dispute over labor unions' attempts to organize the mills. Some five thousand workers gathered at the Labor Temple, then marched in protest to the park.

The city gradually improved the park. Two tennis courts were built in 1927 and were lighted for night play in 1935. By 1938, the park was a major recreation center offering four tennis courts, two volleyball courts, a softball diamond, and a checkers court. It was in 1931 that the park was named after John Clark, one of the city's founding powers, who had died in 1922. On August 11, the park board endorsed a proposal to erect a bronze memorial to Clark.

Parks were the symbol of civic health in the early twentieth century. To promote a city, parks were often displayed on postcards such as this view of City Park in 1914. City Park was later renamed Clark Park.

The Swalwell family was very influential in Everett's early development. Seen here at Swalwell Land, Loan and Trust Office on Chestnut, just south of Hewitt Avenue, beginning with the third man from the right are: G. W. Swalwell, W. G. Swalwell, Wellington Swalwell, Mr. Garrett, and William P. Brown.
King and Baskenville, photographer; Duryee Collection

In June 1946, Clark was designated as the only city park where political and religious gatherings would be permitted. The tennis courts were resurfaced for dancing and roller skating in 1954. By the 1970s, the city had outgrown its first park. The popularity of the concerts waned, and the band shelter was demolished in 1979. The materials were used to build a sauna in Forest Park. In 1981, the city gave the western half of the park to the Everett School District, which built six tennis courts there. A health court was built in 1986, adding fitness fans to the people who enjoy the park's playground, gazebo, and Civil War-era cannon.

This view of Everett looks west on Hewitt past Chestnut.
Everett Public Library

*Everett's first three years saw Henry Hewitt and the Everett
Land Company build a barge work, a nail factory, a paper
mill, a shipyard, a street railroad and a waterworks.*
Frank LaRoche, photographer; Everett Public Library

*Henry Hewitt and his partners in the Everett Land Com-
pany laid the foundation from which Everett grew to a
prominent community.*
Everett Public Library, circa 1890s

A source of entertainment for Everett citizens over the years, the Clark Park bandstand was removed in 1979.

The Civil War era cannon has given Clark Park a very distinctive flavor through the years. It is fitting that Clark Park, Everett's first park, contains a symbol of an even older generation.

Al Weis, the Forest Park zookeeper, stands by Rosie the elephant, given to the zoo by a traveling circus in the late 1940s.

Forest Park

Forest Park was far from the heart of Everett when the city bought it in September 1894. But the two remote five-acre tracts on the south side of Rucker Hill were destined to grow into the city's most popular recreation center. It cost the city less than $10,000 for those first ten acres of forest land. Early Everett people who wanted to spend a few hours in a park probably would have chosen the more developed Clark Park rather than Forest Park, which in those days was called South Park or Swalwell Park, after the family that had owned part of the land.

The depression that began in 1893 made money scarce, and the park remained undeveloped for years. It was used mostly for hunting, fishing, and picnicking. In 1909, the city bought another eighty acres of land from the Swalwell family. The park was formally named Forest Park in 1913, and grew by twenty more acres in 1916. That purchase linked the park to Puget Sound via Pigeon Creek and pretty much established its permanent shape.

Three deer, two coyotes, and two pelicans were given to the city in 1914 by the game warden and were the beginnings of the Forest Park Zoo. During the next few decades, when the park was being run by Oden Hall, brother Walter and nephew John, the zoo boomed. Hall stocked the zoo by using his imagination and relatively little money. He collected young animals from overcrowded parks along the West Coast and in British Columbia. He took occasional gifts from circuses traveling through and he made trades. On a trip to Vancouver, British Columbia, to pick up some Canadian geese, the border authorities wouldn't let Hall back across with his new charges. What to do? The geese were released in Canada, given time to walk over the border unaccompanied, and gathered back into the Halls' truck for the ride to Everett.

The Halls raised food for the birds and other non-carnivorous animals, using their fields in the off season for baseball games. For the meat eaters, the park staff arranged with farmers and highway officials to notify them of dead livestock and road kill.

The zoo was scattered along a pathway that ran down a steep hill. The animal collection varied, but at one time or another during the 1920s included lions, bison, elk, deer, monkeys, zebras, an elephant, bears, goats, coyotes, a badger, raccoons, a rabbit, and a skunk. The zoo had become too expensive by mid-century, and it was scaled back until the zookeeper position was eliminated in April 1958. Three bond issues to upgrade the facilities failed, and in 1962, most of the zoo was torn down. Peacocks continue to

Started in 1914, the Forest Park Zoo was run by Oden Hall, brother Walter, and nephew John. Oden stocked the zoo by using his imagination and relatively little money.

roam freely in the park grounds, and since 1970, the park has offered a popular summer animal farm visited by thousands of children and adults.

This is the Swalwell family homestead. The Swalwells played
an important role in establishing Forest Park. In 1909 they
sold eighty acres to the city to expand the park.
Everett Public Library

Frank and Edward Friday were among Everett's earliest settlers and innovators. Owners of Friday Land Company, they
sold the city the first five acres establishing Forest Park.
Everett Public Library, circa 1890s

For many generations, children have cooled off from the summer sun in the Forest Park wading pool.

The wallaby kangaroo was one of the more exotic creatures to inhabit the Forest Park zoo.

The major thrust of development came during the 1930s as a result of federal programs such as the Works Progress Administration. In the early days, WPA activity in the Everett parks consisted largely of giving people tools and having them clear land and clean parks. By 1937, projects slated for Forest Park included a stadium, baseball and football fields, a fieldhouse and concessions building, trails, roads, and picnic grounds. The WPA sponsored "play days" that attracted as many as three thousand

The old Monkey House at the Forest Park Zoo. The zoo was scattered along a pathway that ran down a steep hill. The animal collection varied, but during the 1920s included lions, bears, bison, zebras, and coyotes.

youngsters for organized games and activities. They offered swimming lessons, archery, a weekly visit by a library book truck, and a "hole in one" tournament. A road was built along upper Pigeon Creek #1 to the beach below on Puget Sound. Floral Hall, the brainchild of the county's Gladiolus Society, was started in 1939. Lumber for the rustic building was specially logged near Three Lakes. The building was finished in time for the society's 1940 gladiolus show. Since then, Floral Hall has been the scene of countless flower shows and other gatherings. When it was remodeled during the 1960s, a dance floor was added.

Development was sporadic after the WPA was discontinued. In 1951 the Skiers Club built a ski jump in the park, and extended it the following year. It was later abandoned. The Everett Community College carpentry class built a concession building in 1963, and a recreation building and a picnic shelter in 1965. The Parks and Recreation Department headquarters building was built in the park in 1967, when the headquarters were moved out of City Hall.

A park master plan was completed in 1971 and updated in 1989 to coordinate development in the park. The zoo's old butcher shop and the land around it became the animal farm in 1970. In 1986 the Lions Club helped refurbish a World War II portable building that is used for meetings.

One of the jewels in Everett's park system is the Forest Park Swim Center. The first splashes were heard in the million-dollar pool in 1976. The fabric roof was destroyed by a storm and replaced with a permanent structure in 1984.

Today's Forest Park is a major regional center with more than 110 acres and excellent recreation facilities. It houses the Parks and Recreation Department, making it the nerve center of the entire park system. As the 1980s end, the park's future is as bright as its playground in May.

Summer fun in Forest Park.
Everett Herald

Planting trees on the hillside in Forest Park was one of the many WPA projects that helped fashion Everett's parks in the 1930s.
Everett Public Library

John Hall was appointed superintendent from 1956 to 1972, following the resignation of his father, Walter, who had served as superintendent since 1939. John's, Uncle Oden Hall, served as park superintendent from 1921 to 1938.

A Forest Park gardener clearing out the greenhouse in order to make pre-winter repairs, fall 1957.
Everett Herald

21

Floral Hall was built by the Works Progress Administration in 1939-1940. One of the first events to be held in Floral was the Snohomish County Gladiolus Show.

In the early 1940s, citizens could enjoy the well kept English Gardens in Forest Park. It was a beautiful place to have a picnic and enjoy the scenery.

The Kiddie Korral in Forest Park was a popular play area for Everett's children in the 1950s and 1960s.

The bears at Forest Park and their cage were relocated to the Olympic Game Range in 1974. For years a visit to the Forest Park bears was a weekly routine for many families. Juleen, photographer

The Sunken Garden can still be enjoyed today at Floral Hall in Forest Park.

The Everett Police Department presents a prize to a little girl during Playday in Forest Park in 1956.
Everett Herald

Community groups, such as these people enjoying themselves at the Home Demonstration Picnic at Forest Park, frequently used park facilities for their gatherings.
Ray Watters, photographer; *Everett Herald*

Grand Avenue Park Way, Everett, Wash.
"The City of Smokestacks."

Grand Avenue Park in 1910 was the third park developed by the city. A spectacular view of the bay can be seen from this park.
F. H. Nowell, photographer; Helen Jackson Collection

Grand Avenue Park

*"On the beach
near this spot
Vancouver
landed June 4, 1792"*

The granite marker so inscribed was put in place 123 years later by the Marcus Whitman Chapter, Daughters of the American Revolution, in a town called Everett. Captain George Vancouver never stood on the bluff. The solid reminder at Grand Avenue Park is meant to approximate the location of his visit.

It was the captain, of course, who sailed into these waters, claimed and named Puget Sound after his young naval lieutenant, Peter Puget, and went on to name Port Gardner Bay and Port Susan after Sir Alan Gardner and his lady. History has it that the English explorer was fascinated by the place. He should have climbed the bluff. Despite what must have been a voyage of adventure and beauty for Vancouver in the late 1700s, he could have added from this outlook a memorable view. Facing the bay from Grand Avenue Park remains an invigorating experience today. Then, the water was nearer to the bluff. Landfills extending into the bay were far in the future. Arriving through the forest, the view from the bluff must have been spectacular.

The native Snohomish tribe knew this place. The rough, stumped and struggling city preserved it, with a park created in 1906. Thirteen years after the city was established, twelve years after Clark and Forest parks were created, land for the Grand Avenue Park was sold to the city by the Everett Improvement Company for

the legal fee of $1. Company President John T. McChesney signed the quit claim deed. Grand Avenue Park lay on three and a half acres between what are now Sixteenth and Nineteenth streets. From the Snohomish River Bridge to the west boundary of the Great Northern Railway Company's right of way following the shoreline below, to the south boundary of Shaffer's First Addition to Everett, a valuable strip of land became public domain.

It was 1911 when William C. Butler's home was built across from the park. Butler was an Easterner of intellect and determination who came West to manage the Rockefeller interests in Everett. That many of his fellow citizens found him cold and proud was apparently of little concern or consequence to Butler. He stayed to become a dominant banker and city leader until his death in 1944. The home he built on the bluff remains one of the city's finest. A 1914 postcard of the park shows a peaceful, green place much like the park today. And the need for such a pretty place is noted in the card's inscription: Everett, Washington, "The City of Smokestacks."

It helps to remember that this was once a positive concept. The early industrialists responsible for the smokestacks saw the sense of park land. Working people, they must have rea-

The home of the late Senator Henry Jackson and his family overlooks Grand Avenue Park. Originally built by William Butler in 1911, the home has a spectacular view of the Puget Sound.
Everett Public Library

soned, need a place for recreation. The park became a daily part of the many millworkers' trek to their homes from their work at the Clark-Nickerson lumber and planing mills below. The Nineteenth Street steps were one of three sets down the bluff.

But all was not idyllic. In the lumber and shingle mills and logging camps, workers were at odds with owners. By 1916, disputes between the unions and the mill owners erupted in the infamous Everett massacre. The IWW, Industrial Workers of the World, or "Wobblies," fought head-on as they tried to land a ship from Seattle packed with union men. It isn't known who fired the first shot, but when the fighting was over, more than fifty men on shore and ship were wounded or dead. The battle waged below the bluff. Labor strife was muted by World War I in 1917. Everett focused its collective thought on national issues.

Late in August of 1923, lights were installed at the park. Park stairs continued to carry workers to their jobs. During the Depression years, men rode freight trains to new parts of the country, hoping to find work. When they landed in Everett, they often climbed the stairs in search of a hot meal.

By the 1960s, the last of the stairs were decrepit and overgrown. It was well past the time when riding the rails was honest work. Unsavory sorts who had hopped a freight to reach Everett were climbing the steps to the park. They weren't welcome. The stairs were eventually removed.

William Butler was originally sent to Everett to assess the Rockefeller investments. He stayed on after Rockefeller cancelled his investments and became a highly respected and successful banker.
Everett Public Library

In April 1961, picnic tables were removed because neighbors had complained. Benches remained facing the water. A new sidewalk was added in 1964.

When Sen. Henry M. Jackson and his wife, Helen, moved to the old Butler house at 1703 Grand Avenue in 1968, Grand Avenue Park looked just about the way it looks today. From the Jackson library windows, the park and Port Gardner Bay beyond offer a peaceful view. The Jackson children, Annamarie and Peter, grew up with the park across the street. "When they were little, we'd pack a little lunch and go over," Helen Jackson said. "I remember someone gave Peter a camera when he was about ten. He took a whole roll of sunsets from the park." Today, when

One of Everett's first parks, Grand Avenue Park was created in 1906. Located across the street from the late Senator Henry M. Jackson's home, the park has a sweeping view of Puget Sound.

she has house guests, Jackson often puts them in Peter's childhood room to enjoy the spectacular view. When "Scoop" was alive, he loved to show visitors the view, Helen Jackson recalled. "Especially people from back East," she said.

Today, Grand Avenue Park is a busy place, as Jackson confirms. There are no swings, picnic tables, or exercise bars. Rather, this is a place to stroll, jog, eat lunch on a blanket, or watch the horizon. Occasionally, neighbors say, someone finds it a tranquil spot to be married. There is little to detract from the grand view. The quiet English garden continues in a setting created simply as a beautiful place to behold the past, and envision the future. Captain Vancouver would have loved it.

The Everett waterfront at the turn of the century attracted
Frederick Weyerhaeuser and his associates.
Everett Public Library

Chapter 2

Mini Parks

J. J. Hill Park
Judd and Black Park
Maggies Park
Bridle Park

J. J. Hill Park

James J. Hill was known as the Empire Builder, partly because he built the Great Northern Railroad from the Midwest to the Pacific Coast. But the nickname also fit because his railroad encouraged the settling and development of the vast lands it crossed, including Everett. When the depression of 1893 drove many investors out of the city, Hill moved in. He bought the wreckage of the Rockefeller interests and formed the Everett Improvement Company. He and partner John McChesney attracted Frederick Weyerhaeuser, Hill's neighbor in St. Paul, to build a lumber mill. Another Hill associate, David Clough, moved West and brought with him relatives and friends who founded a large number of mills and other forest-related businesses. By 1910, there were ninety-five manufacturing plants in Everett, thanks largely to Jim Hill and his promotions.

When Hill's railroad entered downtown Everett, the tracks crossed under a bridge at Hewitt Avenue, then turned left to cross under Broadway and enter the tunnel to Bayside on the west edge of the city. The curve between the two bridges left a small lot on the northeast corner of the intersection of Hewitt and Broadway. The spot was soon home to a tavern called My Office.

The tavern building was torn down in 1975 when Burlington Northern exchanged the property for some city land.

In May 1976, the city council asked the park board to name the property James J. Hill Park. That came as a surprise to the park board, which hadn't been informed that a new park was being created. Original plans for a visitor center were replaced with a proposal for a "green spot" in the business neighborhood. The local unit of the Air National Guard and the Lions Club donated labor and grass seed. The city provided topsoil, plants, and an irrigation system. On April 12, 1977, the park board accepted the project, "with the exception of the name J. J. Hill, or indeed any name at all."

The name stuck anyway, and in 1989 the park is a pleasant green spot in the midst of the heavy urban traffic.

Frederick Weyerhaeuser came to Everett in 1899 when he was contacted by James J. Hill, an old St. Paul friend. Weyerhaeuser eventually built the largest lumber mill in the world.
Weyerhaeuser Archives

The Great Northern locomotive, seen here circa 1912, became a common sight thanks to James J. Hill's investment in Everett.
J. A. Juleen, photographer;
Everett Public Library

30

Located in downtown Everett, J. J. Hill Park is a pleasant green spot in the midst of heavy urban traffic.

James J. Hill was known as the "Empire Builder." His influence was instrumental in Everett's development.
Minnesota Historical Society

The construction of the Great Northern yard in 1902 was an economic boost to the community.
Kirk and Seely, photographers; Everett Public Library

When Everett was created it was envisioned as the "Pittsburg of the West" and the "City of Smokestacks." By 1941 Everett had become more than the mill town of early visionaries, as the Weyerhaeuser Mill by moonlight shows.
Everett Public Library

Judd and Black Park is informally named after a local appliance store located nearby.

Judd and Black Park

A little less than a half-acre between Hewitt Avenue and Maple Street makes up one of three mini parks in Everett. Different from the city's other two mini parks, Maggie's Park and James J. Hill Park, the history here is short.

This Riverside neighborhood itself is steeped in history, but the park is the result of more recent progress. Like Summit Park in the same neighborhood, this park was created when Interstate 5 came to town in the 1970s. And like Summit, the land on which the park sits is still owned by the state of Washington Highway Commission.

It isn't much of a park, really. It wasn't meant to be. When the wedge of land was left behind after freeway construction at the Hewitt Avenue interchange, the city of Everett designed the landscaping simply as a pleasant-looking green space at the eastern entry into town. They added a few benches for lunch-hour visitors or passers-by.

The state used its construction contractor to build the park. When it was complete, in March 1971, the city agreed to maintain it. The park is commonly called Judd and Black Park, although the name isn't official. It refers to the nearby appliance store that has been located in this neighborhood since 1963. Original owner Don Black was said to have delivered the first electric range and refrigerator in Snohomish County in about 1926. At that time appliances were sold through the power company, and Black worked for Puget Sound Power and Light Company in Everett. Wayne Judd was also with Puget Power and had more than twenty years' experience repairing appliances when he and Black went into business together in 1939.

Bob Long, Sr., went to work for Judd and Black fresh out of the Navy after World War II. Beginning as an electrical apprentice, Long took over the business in 1975, then sold it to his sons Bob Jr. and Bill in 1986. In 1988, the company was said to be the largest independent appliance dealer in the state. Customers to the busy appliance store rarely realize there's a park nearby. It's quiet with the exception of a few overflow visitors attracted by the Everett Gospel Mission in the same building.

A young family enjoys an autumn walk in Judd and Black Park

Maggies Park

As the Snohomish River nears Puget Sound, it flows against a ridge of land, turning north to round the ridge and then west again, forming the peninsula where Everett began.

Years before the city was settled, Dennis Brigham made a home on the peninsula's western shore. A tiny corner of his homestead remains as a park. Brigham arrived at his new home from Whidbey Island before the census of 1862, while the peninsula was mostly wilderness and still part of Island County. The land was thickly forested and largely untouched by humans. By all accounts, Brigham liked living alone in his vast parkland, but he remained active in the community. On March 19, 1872, Brigham was granted a homestead certificate for 160.15 acres by President U. S. Grant. He built a cabin on a bluff above the beach and planted an orchard. Brigham sold his homestead for $900 on April 11, 1882, reserving two acres in a lifetime lease. The buyer, in turn, sold the claim in 1890 to the Rucker brothers, who were buying up land to found the city of Everett.

The Ruckers joined up with Henry Hewitt of Tacoma and several Eastern financiers, including John D. Rockefeller, Colgate Hoyt, and Charles Colby. Brigham's homestead became part of their original Plat of Everett filed February 6, 1892, under the Everett Land Company. In the development process, Brigham's paradise gave way to industry. A century after Brigham's certificate was signed, his old homestead looks out over a busy log harbor, Burlington Northern Railroad tracks running north and south, the Scott Paper plant, and the *Everett Herald* building. A tiny corner of Brigham's land had been set aside as the right-of-way for the foot of Everett Avenue, but was never developed.

In the early 1970s, Maggie Lamus, a member of the park board, decided that the site had become a neighborhood eyesore: "Every year it would be full of political campaign signs, and it was used as a dumping ground for garden refuse," she said. "That area always bothered me. It was the era when other cities were developing mini parks, and I wondered if we couldn't take it over and clean it up."

In 1972, with material donated by Scott Paper, the land was turned into a park with berms and shrubs to shield it from the street. Park board members referred to the project as Maggies Park, and the name was picked up in city records and during dedication ceremonies by Mayor Robert Anderson. It's not official, but the park has been called Maggies ever since.

Everett school children learn about local history during their grade school years. Karen Carpenter's third grade class at Whittier Elementary School was so excited about their study of Dennis Brigham, Everett's first settler, that they wrote this letter to Mayor Bill Moore.

916 Oakes
Everett, WA 98201
May 24, 1989

Dear Mayor Moore,

Our third grade class at Whittier has been studying early Everett history and we learned about Dennis Brigham the first settler also known as "dirty plate face." We think he should have a plaque honoring him as the first settler of Everett. Because this is the year of Washington's Centennial and soon will be Everett's birthday we think it would be appropriate to place a plaque in the park where he first lived. If you do not have the money for this project we would be willing to recycle cans and papers to pay for it. Our class would be very happy and proud to see this plaque in the small park honoring our first settler, Mr. Brigham.

Please let us know if you approve of our idea. We can be contacted at Whittier School during the day. Thank you for reading our letter.

Meagan	Cassie	Alisha
Timothy	Noah	Katie
Christine	Brook	Melissa Stearns
Heidi	Logan	Derek
John	Sunshine	Jania
Sean	Elizabeth	Betsy Johnson
Elizabeth	Jason	Lisa
Moonique	Khang-Nguyen	

P.S. We think Everett is the best place to live!

Bridle Park

When the Bridle Park Addition in southwest Everett was platted in 1955, Pope and Talbot, Incorporated, deeded a piece of land there to the property owners to be used for recreation.

A rugged ravine of something more than an acre, it lies there today, at the back edge of the homes that were developed in the ensuing years. Located east of Mukilteo Boulevard and south of Sound Avenue, just inside the Everett city limits, Bridle Park is for the future.

Now known as Maggies Park, this area was once part of Dennis Brigham's original homestead.

Rucker Avenue as it appeared in the late 1920s.
Juleen, photographer; Everett Public Library

Chapter 3

Neighborhood Parks

Rucker Hill Park
Doyle Park
Edgewater Park
Kiwanis Park
Lions Park
Summit Park
View Ridge Park
Wiggums Hollow Park
Alder Street Park

Rucker Hill Park

Of all the things with the Rucker name on them, Rucker Hill Park is probably the least known. The hill where the park rests is legendary in early Everett history. Rucker Hill and the mansion atop it reach back to the city's roots. Rucker Avenue, too, has traveled through time in the north end of town. Even the Rucker tomb, where eight Ruckers and Armstrongs rest in Evergreen Cemetery, has a reputation of its own. Compared to these, the park is a smaller, quieter reminder.

Just more than three-quarters of an acre encircled by Laurel Drive, Rucker Hill Park is a tiny

39

remnant of this pioneer family who once owned the entire hill. Wyatt and Bethel Rucker were the sons of Jane Rucker. Together they came to Everett from Ohio in the late 1880s. Wyatt remained a bachelor. It was Bethel's wife, Ruby Brown Rucker, and their children, Margaret Rucker Armstrong and Jasper Rucker, who donated land for this neighborhood park on the family's namesake hill.

Park Superintendent Walter Hall received the deed dated May 12, 1954. In presenting the gift, the Ruckers' only requirements were that the property be kept up as a public park or playing field and that it carry the Rucker name. Money for maintenance was a concern to the city at first. In this Eisenhower year of 1954, a Gallup Poll reported that a family of four could live on $60 a week. But in November, in Everett, a levy to raise $65,000 for parks failed to receive voter approval. In the years since, the cost of maintaining this small property has proved to be minimal. And, for the children of the area, the park has offered a fine place to play in a neighborhood that has become dense with homes.

Rucker Hill Park is tucked among the homes on the hill. The grassy playfield looks like the bowled lawn of an estate. Flagstones define a sloped garden area that runs around half of the park's perimeter. Two picnic tables and a wooden sign are the only indications that this isn't just the lawn of a home.

From the park's viewpoint, it's clear why the Ruckers built here in the beginning. Although the family only lived in the Rucker mansion for a few years, the house that Wyatt and Bethel built for their mother has held their name over time. The park that Bethel's wife and children donated to the city in 1954 promises to do the same.

The Rucker Mansion, one of the lasting landmarks of the Rucker family, is now home to former mayor Joyce Ebert and her husband, Dr. J. W. Ebert.
Everett Public Library, 1925

Everett citizens can use Rucker Park to play a quick game of soccer. Others use it for more peaceful pursuits such as reading a book or sunbathing.

Rucker Hill Park was donated to the City on May 12, 1954. The Rucker's only requirements were that the property be kept as a public park and that it carry the Rucker name.
Everett Herald, 1955

EVERETT HARBOR. SHOWING OLYMPIC RANGE.

An artist's vision of Everett as a major port city north of San Francisco Bay as viewed from the original Brigham homestead, later developed into Maggies Park.
Everett Public Library, circa 1892, original from the Duryee Collection.

The Rucker Tomb is a well known symbol of the Rucker Family. Over the years, many people have visited the Evergreen Cemetery to view the 46-foot-high structure.
Everett Public Library

Alder Street Park

In June 1950, the Everett Development Company dedicated the .8 acre lot to the property owners in View Ridge Addition Number Three for park purposes. The city maintains it as a neighborhood park. It has swings, a play area, and open space.

Doyle Park

The sign at the entrance looks like a child must have had a hand in it. No wonder. A child did.

At Thirty-fifth Street and Grand Avenue in Everett's Port Gardner Neighborhood, a park fills the gulch. And the old sign placed there in honor of a seven-year-old boy still greets visitors. These eighteen years later, his name identifies the place for a new generation of kids. This is "Doyle's Park," the sign says. Doyle Cates lived just around the corner in 1971. But the park's story begins years before Doyle was born, when the town itself was young.

The land originally belonged to William Howarth. His home at 3330 Grand Avenue was the showpiece of the estate. Family records indicate that William and Margaret Howarth moved to the house about 1914. It sat just north of the rhododendron-lined driveway and next to the current house at 3324 Grand Avenue. The area south of the driveway, where Doyle Park is today, held gardens, a greenhouse, and tennis court. It was first cultivated as an orchard, then made into a putting green. Later, inspired by their friends the Butcharts, who were renowned for their gardens in Canada, the family began the expansive gardens that became their signature.

Fewer than ten years later, in 1924, Margaret Howarth died.

Ada Howarth Pilz, the eldest of three daughters, moved with her husband William into the house next door at 3324 Grand Avenue. But when William Howarth died in 1937, his family couldn't bear to have someone else live in the original home, and so the house at 3330 Grand was torn down in the years before World War II. The Pilzes took over the Howarth land and expanded the gardens as well.

In the years after the war, caring for the gardens was not easy. Ada and William Pilz donated the one-and-a-half-acre garden area to the Everett School District on July 18, 1951. Shortly afterward, when William Pilz died, the home at 3324 Grand was donated to General Hospital.

Today, Everett Port Commissioner Nina O'Neil and her family live in the former Pilz home. "We bought it from the hospital," O'Neil said. "I have some pictures, just before World War II. The Pilzes owned to 35th Street—the whole gully. It was simply gorgeous, gorgeous gardens."

The trees planted as saplings on both sides of Thirty-fifth Street in Howarth's day meet overhead now, and squirrels play around their trunks. Huge holly bushes from the original landscaping line the west side of the street. The creek at the bottom of the ravine still runs all the way to the bay.

It was in December 1971 that the school district and the city of Everett began a joint venture here. Though the district still owned the property, the city offered to build a playground with government funds.

The playground was designed and built by young people working for the city through the Neighborhood Youth Corps and the federal Employment Security Program. The average age of the construction crew was seventeen. Paul O'Neil, Nina's son, volunteered to lead the crew, according to neighbor Steve Burr. The crew got creative with long structures and upright concrete culverts for climbing and tunnels for crawling.

Doyle Cates and a lot of other neighborhood kids were in their glory watching the new construction. Doyle's mother, Juanita Cates, remembers that her son would bring home chunks of scrap concrete and nails from the site.

Over the years, the grown-up neighbors worked too. They cleared overgrown berry bushes and planted more than two thousand trees in the park and throughout the ravine. "We had work parties on Saturdays, older folks working side by side with younger kids," Burr recalled. The new park equipment lasted as long as Doyle Cates' childhood. He moved from the neighborhood when he was fourteen.

In 1984, the school district found the park property was more than it could afford to maintain. They offered the city of Everett a ten-year lease at $1 a year in exchange for maintenance and upkeep on the park. The lease was authorized by the school board on July 23, 1984. The city council voted to accept the ten-year lease August 4, 1984, and agreed to oversee the maintenance with the help of volunteer labor from the Port Gardner Neighborhood Association.

Doyle is a neighborhood park, with a minimal amount of play equipment. The grassy field, though, is just as good for a ball game as it ever

Over the years the cooperative efforts of the View Ridge neighborhood and the Parks Department have provided a pleasant place for the neighborhood children to play.

was. Soccer games are natural in this dished area where the ball can't roll too far away. And in the winter, neighborhood children still slide down the slope on sleds or pieces of cardboard.

Doyle Cates is twenty-five now and still lives in Everett. By happenstance, his name is linked with the history of the city and with its pioneers. The Howarth name is on another, much larger park to the south. And Doyle Park is child's play for a new generation.

View Ridge Park

View Ridge Park is in the city, but it's not really a city park. The Everett Parks Department maintains the playfield for the neighborhood. But it's the homeowners in the neighborhood who own the property. Howard Sievers and George Duecy platted the area in 1944. It was then that two acres at Olympic Boulevard between View Ridge Drive and Park Place were dedicated for park or playground purposes. It's a pleasant place to play. There's a sand-lot ballfield, a basketball area, plus open air and running space tucked together in a shallow, grassy

bowl with flowering plum trees around the rim.

Back in August 1958, some members of the View Ridge Community Club discussed transferring the property to the city. Questions were raised about the title, since all the neighborhood property owners share equally in the management. No decision was reached. In September that year, the parks department relocated drains and graded to provide the View Ridge Community Club Playfield with better drainage.

In February 1959, a neighborhood representative approached the park board about the city acquiring title to the playfield. A decision was made that the title would remain in the neighborhood, but the city agreed to cooperate in the maintenance of the property. By 1964, the field was in need of restoration. Members of the Everett Junior Chamber of Commerce worked on the project that summer with the help of park employees. When work was finished in August, the city agreed to continue maintaining the park.

Children have grown, others have moved in and out of the neighborhood, but over the years the cooperative efforts of the View Ridge Community Club and the city have continued to make View Ridge Park a pleasant place to play.

View Ridge Park is a perfect place for a quick pick-up game of softball among friends.

Overlooking the putting green at Doyle Park to the home of William and Ada Pilz, daughter of William Howarth
Everett Public Library

Edgewater Park

At the far southwestern corner of Everett, across a ravine from the Mukilteo city limits, there was a one-acre tract that was swamp on one end and a cow pasture on the other. In the mid-1930s the community heard that the tract had been earmarked as the site of an auto wrecking yard. Two neighbors, Leo Loken and Art Sorrenson, put an end to any such plans by buying the land.

The community organized the Edgewater Playfield Association, and Loken and Sorrenson donated the property to it. The group built a running track along the perimeter and a fieldhouse in the late 1930s. The fieldhouse was heavily used during World War II for many activities, including dances. When the war ended the building was demolished and replaced by a tennis court.

Edgewater Park is the western gateway to the city of Everett. Recently the neighborhood met with Park staff to re-masterplan the park.

Kiwanis Park

In 1940, the city acquired property at Thirty-sixth Street and Rockefeller Avenue from the county for $6 through a tax title sale that stipulated the property must be used for a playground. The Everett Kiwanis Club provided materials and labor to build a small ball field, later closed because children kept chasing loose balls into the street.

In 1971 there was a flurry of activity at the park. The city council budgeted $40,000 for improvements and officially adopted the name Kiwanis Playfield. By the late 1980s the playfield surface had been painted with sand and sprinkled with several pieces of brightly painted playground equipment. There also is a bicycle rack, a perimeter walkway and, on any pretty day, a large number of gleeful children.

Kiwanis Park, shown here in the 1970s, has changed over the years but it is still a popular neighborhood park where children come to play.

Renovated in 1989, Kiwanis Park is one of Everett's many neighborhood parks.

Lions Park

You can't miss the pale green water tower across the street from Lions Park. It's a good landmark if you're looking for this neighborhood park, and a good reminder of the park's early history. The original three acres here were owned by the Public Utilities Department and operated as the Beverly Park Water System. There were two wooden water towers in the early days. The newer steel tank, which still stands, was built in the 1950s.

Today, Lions Park occupies a bit more than four acres in the South Everett neighborhood of Beverly Park. The land is owned by the city, having been acquired in pieces in the early 1970s. A rolling piece of green borders Seventy-fifth Street on the north, Olympic Drive on the west, and Cascade Drive on the east. The park sits on the north side of the barn-red South Everett Youth Community Center.

Development of the park began in 1972, the same year the swimming pool was started at Forest Park. A name for the park came earlier. For years, the Lions had provided money for projects to benefit the children of Everett. To recognize the work of the South Everett Lions Club, as well as the time and effort the club had devoted to the betterment of the city in general, the city council agreed in June 1971 to name the park "South Everett Lions Park."

In spring 1975, drainage and sod were put in. A wooden fence with chain link and bleachers were added to the ball field. Play areas, restrooms, and a grassy amphitheater were also built.

When it opened officially on June 11, 1975, Lions was the only park in the area. The park today has playground equipment, horseshoe pits, a ball field, basketball hoops, restrooms, and open space.

A playground is planted in sand. Its highlight is a tall fort for climbing by thick log steps or rugged wooden ladders. At the top, a spiral slide offers an exit. Evergreen, fruit and leafy deciduous trees shade the park. There are picnic tables and bike racks. An asphalt path runs throughout the park.

Lions Park is a pretty little place. Although just four acres, the park has room for both active and quiet recreation.

On a sunny, summer day, barefooted children climb the log ladder and squeal down the spiral slide, then beg for big pushes on bucket-seated swings.

The basketball hoops are here for a friendly pickup game, or to fill a lonesome day when a kid finds no one to play. It's no longer used to quench Everett's water needs, but even so, the place is every bit as refreshing as it ever was.

Summit Park

Progress dug a trench through the early Everett area known as Riverside. When Interstate 5 roared through east Everett in the late 1960s, blocks of Harrison Avenue came down to make way for north and southbound traffic. So did all the old homes on the east side of Summit Avenue between Twentieth and Twenty-fourth Streets.

After the bulldozers, the road graders, and the concrete trucks drove away, the Washington State Highway Commission built a park. And when the dust cleared, there was a strip of green on the freeway hillside. At Summit Avenue and Twentieth Street, a two-acre strip of land became a neighborhood park that rises above the hurrying traffic. Summit Park is a green place where neighborhood children play. There are several picnic tables and benches, and room to stroll and take in the view. To the east, the Cascade Mountains are magnificent. The Snohomish River is seen widening, near now to the bay. In the freeway's southbound lanes, green highway signs announce the "City Center" exit and a route to Stevens Pass. The sign to the north shows Marysville, 5 miles; Mount Vernon, 32; and Vancouver, British Columbia 113. The Burlington Northern Railroad makes tracks in the distance.

Quiet today, in contrast to the freeway, the tracks are a reminder of Everett's past. Freeways are to modern times what railroads were to the early 1900s. "This end of town was where the Great Northern Railroad first came in," Summit neighbor Mildred Neff recalled. "This whole area was built for the railroad executives." Neff remembers the neighborhood before the freeway. "I've been here since 1941," she said. In the '40s, Neff lived with her family on Summit. Her girlhood home was one of those taken down for the freeway.

Today, Neff and her husband, John, are just up the street from the site of her first home. "We've lived in this house since 1950," she said. "We raised our three children here." The Neffs' turn-of-the-century home commands a view of the city on the west and the park and the Cascades on the east. State contractors built the park, and lighting and upkeep became the city's

Lions Park bursts with activity during a sunny summer day.

Summit Park was built on excess land from the Interstate 5 Freeway project. Today it is a pleasant greenbelt that the community can enjoy.
Jill Neff, photographer

job in an agreement signed in 1971 by Mayor Robert Anderson.

As the Snohomish River gouged land in its progress to the sea, so the freeway found a passage for traffic through Everett. Yet neighborhood children sheltered by the park's greenbelt are oblivious to the past and unperturbed by the hurry below. They neither know nor care that the place where they play is the result of progress. Their playfield is grass sprinkled with daisies and dandelions.

51

Wiggums Hollow Park

In the spring of 1969, county and city governments got together to build a neighborhood park for Grandview Homes. Parents in the housing project had proposed the idea and asked that the play area be completed by the time school was out that summer.

Through the cooperative efforts of the Community Action Council, the Inter-Church Committee for Social Action, the city, county, and the parents a park was built. When it was finished, the park was turned over to the city for management. But the first setting just didn't work. The five acres at 2808 Tenth Street in north Everett across from the Charles Denny Youth Center were originally a Snohomish County park. In the joint venture agreement between the county and city parks departments, the county supplied the land, the earthwork, and the landscaping. Together, city and county agreed to make further improvements, and the city agreed to maintain the property.

It was given a wonderful name. Wiggums Hollow honors Hawthorne Elementary School Principal Arnold Wiggum for his involvement in the neighborhood. By the time the kids at Hawthorne were out of school in the summer of 1969, a temporary playfield had been created as the parents had hoped. Major work began in the summer of 1972.

Hills, tunnels, sand piles, caves, and other land formations were designed into the playground. Permanent playground equipment, picnic tables, restrooms, and a Navy A4D jet, from the aircraft carrier *Kittyhawk,* were installed.

Then the problems began to show. Maintenance was difficult from the beginning, made worse by a shortage of personnel. More important, the park was designed as a large play area without provisions that would encourage families. During the 1970s, the park was all but destroyed by vandals. In summer 1977, redesign was considered. City and county meetings found that the park had been poorly conceived and did not serve the needs of its neighbors. Joe Kozlovski submitted a proposed plan to Park Director Chuck Logan to eliminate the mound areas, fill in the tunnel, level the area, eliminate some play equipment viewed as dangerous and install new play equipment. Total cost to redevelop the facility was about $165,000.

The park was renovated during the late 1970s in cooperation with the Greater Riverdale Association. By 1979, all structures had been removed and the park was regraded and seeded in 1980. The changes allowed for picnicking, walking, playground activities, and a greenbelt area.

In September 1983, the county transferred the Wiggums Hollow property to the city. An additional acre of land previously owned by the Everett Housing Authority was added to Wiggums Hollow in 1987.

Change continues. In 1988, hydro seeding and irrigation were completed. A volleyball/basketball court, new playground equipment, paved pathways, and facilities for the elderly and the handicapped were built. Today, by design, picnic tables and barbecues, playground equipment and walkways encourage park use by all ages.

Wiggums Hollow was built in 1960 through the cooperative efforts of the Community Action Council, the Inter-Church Committee for Social Action, City of Everett, Snohomish County, and neighborhood parents.

Wiggums Hollow of the 1980s is a popular play area for children in the surrounding neighborhoods.

Silver Lake City Beach has been a part of Everett's recreational programs since the 1920s. Many citizens have enjoyed swimming and picnicking along its shores.

Chapter 4

Beaches

Thornton A. Sullivan
Silver Lake Park
Howarth Park
Everett Beaches

Thornton A. Sullivan
Silver Lake Park

Even in Everett's early days Silver Lake was called "the beauty spot of Snohomish County." It is a place where calm blue water reflects the sun. There is room for fishing, boating, and watching the ducks go by. The lake was far south of the city but it had attracted small scale development by 1912, when the county was offered 46.5 acres of heavily timbered land on the shore for $300 an acre. The county commissioners thought about the proposal, but it wasn't until 1919 that city planners tried to sell bonds to pay for the park's development. In June 1920, with the land bought by the bonds still not sold, the park board decided to go ahead with plans for a bathhouse and beach. By that time, Silver Lake was already a popular place during the summer. The YMCA taught swimming there, and lots of businesses, fraternal groups, and trade organizations used it for picnics.

The name Everett Silver Lake Park was chosen from among names suggested by schoolchildren, and dedication ceremonies were held in March 1922. From 1941 to 1946, the Army Air Corps leased Silver Lake Park as a recreational area for troops from Paine Field. The commanding officer, Colonel A. C. Strickland, said the park would be open to the public so that the troops could socialize with civilians. But a year later another commanding officer, A. A. Yotz, was holding daily formal parades and reviews there and the park became as much a military installation as a park. When the Army left, the park was in bad shape. In April 1946, the park board granted the Old Everett Gun Club a three-year lease to develop a shooting range, but for the most part the park was unused. Little happened until Frank Patterson arrived on the scene in January 1949.

Patterson was the Everett police officer in charge of the city's school safety patrol, the students who directed children at intersections on their walk to school. In 1948 the Everett youngsters had been treated to a camp sponsored by the State Patrol at Deception Pass on Whidbey Island. Patterson wanted something closer to home, and the park board gave him access to Silver Lake. The park board may have been a little surprised at the whirlwind of activity that resulted. Patterson started with the lake, the land, and whatever deteriorated facilities were left after the Army moved out. The Optimist Club of Everett had recently disbanded and the members donated their treasury balance of $300 to the project.

Patterson, who later became the chief of police, was something of a genius at both promotion and organization. He quickly obtained donations of bricks, lumber, cement, pipe, shingles, paint, veneer, and even trucks to haul the material. During spring vacation, a group of boys moved into tents that had been erected at the park. There were frequent recreation periods, but when the boys weren't playing, Patterson had them working to prepare the site for permanent facilities. They cooked their own meals on outdoor fireplaces.

Personnel from the Air Force arrived to rebuild a rotted bridge, erect three outdoor fireplaces, rebuild a baseball backstop, and build a floating dock. The airmen also arranged to dispose of the camp's refuse throughout the camping season. In return, Air Force people were allowed to swim at the beach. When the boys had prepared the site, three volunteer master carpenters arrived to help build a cook shack, aided by the Everett High School carpentry class. The cook shack was finished in time for the patrol boys' first camp during the summer of 1949. Patterson's wife, Ethel, was the cook.

For the next several years the board was bombarded with reports, suggestions, requests, and statistics from Patterson. In January 1950, Patterson pointed out to the park board that the camp had three permanent buildings without cost to the park department. And so it continued. By 1952, the school patrol boys were using the camp for several week-long periods during the summer. Swimming classes were sponsored by the *Everett Herald* and the Red Cross. The process continued and as Patterson and his volunteers improved the park, it received wider use. In June 1961, the park board named the park the Thornton A. Sullivan Recreation Area, after the board president. In August 1963, a plaque was put in the park to honor the work done by Patterson, who by then was a police captain. The campgrounds in those days were used primarily by organizations that worked with specialized groups such as handicapped youngsters.

By 1966, Park Superintendent John Hall had taken over the supervision of improvements at the park, including installing a diving float. He also arranged with the Everett Junior College carpentry class to build a replacement for the bathhouse and caretaker's cottage.

Through the years, the park acquired canoes and small sailboats which became the basis for large-scale education programs in boating and water safety. The Mariner High School physical education department traditionally used Silver Lake and its boats for sailing classes.

By the mid-1970s, the Silver Lake area was heavily populated. The park board decided to look into buying waterfront property on the lake. In 1978, the Silver Lake Kiwanis Club donated .6 acres to the city, and in October 1981 Dean and Carol Richardson donated another .17 acres. Those were early steps in a long-range proposal to acquire waterfront land circling the lake. The plan was to provide for eventual development of the entire beach area for public recreation.

By the end of the 1980s, Silver Lake had a major regional park with twenty-seven acres devoted to multipurpose courts, boat rental, fishing, a multipurpose field, nature trail, swimming beach, waterfront trails, barbecue grills, picnic shelters and tables, play equipment, bathhouse, community building, parking, restrooms, wheelchair access, day camp area, and a fitness court. None of this has spoiled that original fine beach, where the calm blue water still reflects the bright sun.

The Silver Lake Triathlon is a popular annual event which attracts hundreds of athletes and spectators. The event consists of a one-mile swim, a 13.5-mile bike, and a 5.3-mile run.

During the 1920s and 1930s, the water slide at Silver Lake was the focal point of fun and games.
Everett Public Library

One of our first parks, Silver Lake is visited by over a hundred thousand people each year. Home to the Silver Lake Triathlon, Silver Lake also has swimming, picnicking, playgrounds, walking trails, and sailing lessons.

In the 1950s and 1960s, hydroplane races held during the
Silver Lake Regatta were a major attraction.
Everett Herald

In the 1950s and 1960s Silver Lake was the favorite spot for
people to cool off on hot summer days.

Chief of Police Frank Patterson was instrumental in revital-
izing Silver Lake during the 1950s. Seated are, left to right,
Skip Parker, Sgt. Gene Oswald, and Frank Patterson. Stand-
ing are, left to right, Dale Sabine, Jim Burnette, Bob Young,
and Ted Hazen.
Everett Herald

Camp Hebolb Summer Day Camp at Silver Lake is one of the many children's programs offered by the Parks Department.

Dance, arts, swimming, bowling, Special Olympics, and Camp Patterson Day Camp are special programs for special people.

Howarth Park

In 1916, Everett acquired the city waterworks from Stone and Webster Company, which had established and operated the system from the city's earliest days. Almost immediately the city began developing a huge new water supply in the Sultan River basin in the Cascade Mountains east of the city. When the Sultan development was completed in 1919 the city shut down the Stone and Webster watershed in Pigeon Creek #2 just south of the city. The city kept the land, and in 1941 platted part of it for housing and reserved the rest for a park.

Pigeon Creek took the place of the city beach at Maple Heights until the mid-1950s, when Puget Sound waters became contaminated and the Great Northern Railway moved its tracks onto the land. The land remained largely deserted until 1971, when the city began a new development and named it Howarth Park, after William and Leonard Howarth, part owners of the Everett Pulp and Paper Company mill in Lowell and community activists in the early 1900s.

The early 1970s were desperate times for Western Washington. A recession slashed into the sales of the Boeing Company, the region's industrial giant and by far the largest employer. The company cut its work force from 101,000 in 1968 to 37,000 in 1971. Businesses disappeared, people moved away, and property values plummeted.

Everett was ready for someone to spend hundreds of thousands of dollars, both to build a park and to provide jobs. The plan called for a bulkhead to raise the beach above high tide, a pedestrian overpass at the railroad tracks, foot trails, an overlook, tennis courts, restrooms, a play area, and a large open lawn. Construction began in 1971 with Navy Seabees and youth groups doing some of the work as volunteers. The rest of the Phase I work was done under contract by Parson's Landscaping Company. On October 20, Mayor Robert Anderson presided over a picnic to dedicate the park. The second phase was completed by Newland Construction Company shortly after the first.

In 1973, Howarth Park won an award from the American Society of Landscape Architects. But there were problems brewing. Much of the rustic appearance of the park had been achieved by using rough-hewn wood as the major construction material. The untreated wood rotted. With the region still suffering from "The Boeing crunch," the city had little money available for

City Beach at Howarth Park in the early 1900s.
Everett Public Library

park maintenance. An inventory of the facilities in all the parks in the early 1980s showed the new Howarth Park to be in as poor a condition as the older parks. Under the guidance of park Director Bob Cooper, a new master plan for the park system was developed. The city council and Mayor Bill Moore provided funds for a major recovery program throughout the system, including Howarth Park.

The Howarth recovery program began just in time. In spring 1986, engineers found that the bridge over the railroad tracks was so badly savaged by rot and vandalism that it was in danger of collapsing just from the vibrations of passing trains. It was closed and demolished, and in July 1987 it was replaced by a $240,000 bridge built of materials that would resist both weather and vandals. Elsewhere in the park the city carried out a five-phase renovation program. By the end of the decade much of the recovery program had been carried out, and the park was once again the scene of major recreation programs ranging from tennis to picnicking to beachcombing. In season, there are guided interpretive walks on the trails, in the forest, and at the tidelands. Pigeon Creek #2 has become a well rounded park.

William Howarth (pictured with his family) and his brother, Leonard were community activists in 1900s. Leonard donated $75,000 of the $100,000 needed to build the Everett Library. William gave heavily to youth groups, including the Deaconess Children's Home and many others.
Everett Public Library

*In 1988, the Parks Department had the Howarth Bridge
rebuilt with steel girders.*
Dave Hornor, photographer; *Everett Herald*

Throughout the years, children have enjoyed Everett's beautiful, sandy beaches.

Everett Beaches

By the second decade of the twentieth century, Everett was no longer the solid forest it had been thirty years earlier. The 1910 census counted 24,814 people settled into a stable community of nearly five thousand homes. The bayside beach was lined with mills. To take a dip in Puget Sound, many people walked the Great Northern tracks south past the city.

In fall 1919, the park board proposed to use part of a $50,000 bond issue to develop a public beach at Pigeon Creek. The bond issue passed the voters' test, but was turned back by a Seattle brokerage house on a technicality. The park board decided to put whatever resources it could scrape up into the new Silver Lake Park and, according to a newspaper article on June 8, 1920, the Pigeon Creek beach was put on the shelf.

In 1927, the board shifted its effort to the Maple Heights area about a mile south of the first Pigeon Creek site. In February, delegates from the American Legion agreed with the park board to visit beaches at Maple Heights, Pigeon Creek #2, and the Everett Jetty. These visits led to an agreement to purchase the beach at Maple Heights from the Maple Heights Land Company. A month or so later the park board obtained additional land from the land company and from the Beard and Follestad families, who were related to park Superintendent Oden Hall.

With the land purchased, the board moved on to the job of building a bridge over the Great Northern Railway tracks at Maple Heights. In March 1928, the board awarded a $1,705 contract for the bridge to H. V. Emmons, later adding $300 to drive pilings into an area of quicksand Emmons discovered. The bridge was finished by May 1, and the park board moved on to finishing touches including a bathhouse and a boom to protect it from driftwood. The beach opened early in June with some two hundred swimmers on hand and Cy Wolfe as lifeguard. The American Legion organized a dedication and "jollification" for June 14, with music by the Drum and Bugle Corps. The Maple Heights beach served the city through the 1930s and into the 1940s.

In September 1941, the city leased the Maple Heights Park to the Boy Scouts, who used it until about the end of 1948. During those years, the park board was preparing a replacement beach. In April 1942, it set to work on a thirty-acre tract at Pigeon Creek #2, about a half-mile north of Maple Heights. The Weyerhaeuser

In 1902 mills and shipyards occupied much of Everett's waterfront. Today the Everett Marina expands across the waterfront.
Everett Public Library

Company donated tideland, and city engineer G. G. Paine negotiated with Great Northern for permission to tunnel under its tracks to the beach.

The shortages of World War II were becoming apparent, and building materials were allotted almost entirely to war-related projects. But the park board plunged in to develop Pigeon Creek #2, perhaps reasoning that the new beach would be available to troops of the Army Air Corps base being built at Paine Field.

The beach opened on July 3, 1943, with a bathhouse, concession stands, spectator areas, a cupola, and porches on three sides. There was a cottage nearby for the caretaker, covered picnic spots, and a plan in hand for a playground, a wading pool, and an arboretum. A crossing guard stood at the tracks since the park board was still negotiating on the underpass.

The beach must have been quite the place to be in those next few years. During the 1944 season, which opened on Memorial Day, the Elks Lodge provided free bus rides from the city for children on Tuesdays and Saturdays. By 1952, Everett city buses had service to the beach three times a day, six days a week. On Sundays there were nine buses to Forest Park, and four of them continued on to the beach.

The season's opening in 1953 was delayed because of contamination in the bay water. In 1955 the railroad moved to expand its tracks onto the land occupied by the bathhouse, and the beach was abandoned early in 1956. Pigeon Creek #2 was not again an officially sanctioned recreation area until Howarth Park was developed in 1974, and a bridge over the railroad tracks was built. After years of attacks by nature and vandals, the bridge became unsafe, and it was replaced in 1988. A bulkhead provided a beach above the high tide line, but the long summer days on the bathhouse porch were gone.

Every summer over thirteen thousand visitors board a passenger ferry for Everett's Jetty Island. A man-made island, the Jetty has the best "warm water" swimming in Puget Sound.

Sunbathing on Jetty Island 1963 before the program ended. The program was later renewed with the support of the Port of Everett and continues to be a popular summer program.
Everett Herald

69

Ken Tyson was the golf pro at Legion Memorial Golf
Course from 1956 to 1964. Former golf pros at the course
include: 1937 to 1943, Jack Martin; 1944 to 1953, Ray Glenzer;
1954 to 1955, Ken Tyson; 1956 to 1964, Guy Hupe; 1964 to
1965, Arnie Johnson; and since 1965 Bob Whisman, who
shares time at Walter Hall course.
Ray Watters, photographer, *Everett Herald*

Chapter 5

Memorial Parks

Walter E. Hall Park
and Golf Course
Legion Memorial Park
and Golf Course
Kasch Park

Walter E. Hall Park
and Golf Course

In 1900, Walter E. Hall worked his way to America by shoveling coal into the hungry boilers of a turn-of-the-century steamship. He had no idea that he and two members of his family would become towering figures in the development of Everett's parks, or that he would leave his name on one of the major parks. Hall was a machinist in his native England. After he arrived in New York, he worked for a soap factory and lived in Jersey City, New Jersey. After he established himself, he sent to England for his family, including his wife, parents, brothers, sisters, and the fiances of two of the sisters. His son, John, was born in Jersey City.

About 1911, when John was four, Walter traveled to Alaska. "He got up as far as Valdez and said that wasn't for him," John said many years later. Walter's father and sister were in Everett, so he stopped there and sent for the rest of the family. Walter got a job as a machinist for Sumner Iron Works. His brother, Oden, had been a gardener and greenhouse man in England. Some time after the family arrived in Everett Oden went to work as a gardener for the Hulbert family, who owned one of the large mills on the Everett waterfront.

In about 1920, Oden was appointed assistant to park Superintendent H. W. North. In 1921, he was appointed to the superintendent's position. For the next half century the Hall family supervised, nurtured, developed, and loved the Everett park system.

Throughout all of that period, one of the Halls was serving as superintendent of parks. Often another family member was serving at the same time in another park job. From 1927 to 1930, Oden held the position of park board secretary in addition to being superintendent. He was replaced as secretary by Arthur Paxton but continued as superintendent until his death in 1938.

John had learned gardening from his Uncle Oden and from his grandfather. While he was still in school he started working as a gardener for the Butler family, an experience that helped prepare him for a distinguished career in the city parks. When he graduated from Everett High School, John went to the University of Washington engineering school for two years, then dropped out to get married. He worked a year as a timekeeper at Sumner Iron Works, then went to Alaska for three years as a machinist in a canning factory. After he returned to Everett in the early 1930s he worked for twenty years in Weyerhaeuser's Mill B.

During the 1930s, the Sumner Iron Works had shut down temporarily, throwing Walter Hall out of work. Oden, who had had tuberculosis for years, was becoming increasingly ill, and about 1935 he hired his brother to work in the parks. On July 15, 1937, Walter was officially named assistant to his brother.

During the last days of Oden's tenure he was too ill to perform the duties of the job, and Walter became the acting superintendent. Oden died on December 27, 1938, and the park board voted unanimously on January 10, 1939, to appoint Walter as the new superintendent. John quit his Weyerhaeuser job in 1947 to go to work for his father in the parks. "Dad was getting kind of feeble and wanted me to give him a hand," John said later. John took the civil service exam, and his appointment as a gardener went into

effect on January 9, 1948. In July 1953, he was appointed assistant superintendent in charge of Legion Park, the community center, and the city golf course. Two years later, he became acting superintendent when his father vacated the superintendency. John was named superintendent on May 10, 1956, and held that job until he retired February 1, 1972.

John's tenure saw a change in the public perception of parks in Everett and the nation. Originally, parks were thought of as places set aside for beautiful gardens. The Halls agreed with that proposition. "That is one of the big changes that came to pass during the time I was superintendent," John said. "Recreation began to take over." Years after he retired, he was still not in full approval of that approach. "Wherever recreation took over, the parks went downhill as far as beauty and being a peaceful area," he added.

Everett and Snohomish County were a changing, growing community when John became superintendent. Growth brought both opportunities and demands—for water, supplies, sewers, streets, and parks. It was time for Everett to fix up its existing parks and to add new ones. This was John Hall's challenge, and creating a huge new park and recreation area named after his father was one of his biggest satisfactions. The park is the Walter E. Hall Recreation Area at 1226 West Casino Road. It consists of a 133.13-acre, eighteen-hole golf course, and a nine-acre recreation area.

Plans were approved to develop a clubhouse, mini course, driving range, restaurant, creative-play area, bike trails, tennis courts, picnic area, and restrooms. Most of the facilities were opened when Mayor Bob Anderson dedicated the new park on May 27, 1972. Construction costs were set at $238,623. Dale Dempsey was named as the first golf pro at the course. He was succeeded January 1, 1974, by Bob Whisman. In 1974, the park board voted to form a Junior Golf Association for youngsters and to allow the Cascade High School Golf Team to use the course without charge.

In 1984 the park department made plans to add soccer fields, play equipment, covered picnic benches, and a new picnic shelter. On the golf course, the plan called for a major revamping of the drainage and irrigation equipment, as well as new cart paths, holding ponds, sand traps, tees, and greens. The plan was approved on June 12, 1984, and construction started in 1988.

*Park Supervisor John Hall lends a hand in setting up a
dahlia show in Floral Hall at Forest Park.*

John Hall Park Superintendent and Miss Florina Pink.
Everett Herald

Everett golfers value the efforts of the Parks Department Maintenance crew in keeping the fairways green and in prime playing condition.

Par 3 hole on Walter E. Hall Golf Course is rated one of the most challenging in Snohomish County.

American Legion
Memorial Park

Thick forest covered the peninsula. The cedars and firs grew so dense, nurtured by the soft, steady rains, that in places the sun never touched the ground. Within, the air smelled rich with earth. Fresh water flowed freely, cascading toward the western sea. In return, the wind carried the scent and the sound of the sea to the forest.

In the distance to the north and east, rugged, snow-covered peaks created a boundary. On the west, another line of peninsula mountains formed a backdrop to the bay. Sunsets were glorious, with only the gull as witness. The animals at home here were protected by the forest, nourished by the land and the water.

Legends of the river people say the transformer, Dokuibel, put them here when he came and changed everything. Struck by its beauty, the people understood the bounty and the promise of the place given by the great changer. They called their village Hebolb. The village was near or below where Legion Park is today. We may never be certain exactly where the early Indian village stood. Surprisingly little has been recorded about this important site, and archaeologists who have studied the area debate the location. Evidence and recorded history of the Snohomish tribe suggest Hebolb was on the water at the foot of the bluff. Arrowheads were found on the bluff when the park was being made.

Records of Indian Agent E. A. Starling in 1852 suppose the Snohomish (Sno-ho identified the river, mish meaning people) numbered 250 in locations at the south end of Whidbey Island, on the Snohomish River, the bay, and nearby. Other equally unreliable estimates run upwards to nearly a thousand. Members of the tribe were known to move with the seasons. Hebolb was home to their leaders. They found themselves well provided here. Reeds and rushes from the river marshes made mats and baskets for the village. Cedar trees created dugout canoes and bark for clothing. The tide flats were home to clams, crab, and flounder. This was a fertile hunting ground.

The largest potlatch house in the area was here, and four large cedar houses each some one hundred feet long by forty feet wide were remembered by tribal member Elizabeth Shelton. There were a good number of smaller houses as well.

By 1877, the Snohomish tribe and others had been assigned to the Tulalip reservation some three miles northwest. In 1890, Indian agents at Tulalip reported 443 people from combined tribes. Years later, from 1950 to 1958, an agency for the U.S. Bureau of Indian Affairs returned to the point, housed in a World War II building.

But until the late 1870s, the point was a place known to no more than a few besides the river people. It was then that the townsite around the point began to draw the attention of the adventurous and ambitious. About 1891, the shingle-producing C. A. Blackman Mill was built on the water below and the area came to be known as Blackman's Point. Drive today across the railroad overpass on Marine View Drive northwest of Legion Park and you'll pass over the site of the old Blackman Mill.

And here was the junction of the Snohomish, Skykomish, and Spokane division of the transcontinental railroad with the Seattle & Montana Railroad to Vancouver that reporter Alvin Pettersen remembered.

Reminiscing in the *Everett Daily Herald*, Pettersen wrote: "We youngsters, who spent a good share of our lives near the mouth of the Snohomish River, swimming on the snag-strewn beach or carrying milk to the cookhouse at Blackman's shingle mill, seem to have taken it for granted that that was the way it had always been and there was not reason for asking questions."

The idea of placing a park on the "point" in the north end of town was entertained in the spring of 1929. The year is best remembered as the year of the stock market crash, but that came in the fall. Things were riding high in the spring. And with Forest Park taking care of the needs of the central, south, and southeastern portions of the city, and Riverdale Park filling the needs of the northeast district, the city was looking north for park land.

A. B. and Harriet Clausen provided the first parcel, in 1932, to the American Legion, Earl Faulkner Post. The Everett Improvement Company, with Dan A. Duryee, Jr., as president, also added land. J. L. Rucker was the notary public for the deed in February 1932.

As the *Everett Daily Herald* described things in a 1935 story, "185 acres (were) acquired by the Legion early in the Depression and turned then to the employment of idle men." The blasting began in February 1932. About sixty acres were cleared early on, though many huge stumps remained for years. Then money ran out. The American Legion applied to the Works Progress Administration for park funds in May

A mother and child enjoy a quiet moment at Legion Memorial Park.

1934. WPA workers planted shrubs, graded and completed two baseball diamonds. A shelter, lookout point and picnic grounds were developed.

On October 2, 1935, the American Legion transferred its title of the land to the city. The deed was to be held in escrow for two years. During that time the city was to make improvements, or have the land revert to the Legion. Some of the improvements included the golf course, baseball diamond and six tennis courts. The transfer was made to allow the city to apply for government funds to complete the park. A private entity would not qualify for federal money.

On October 3, 1935, the city council officially accepted the transfer and sought WPA funds for a playground. Before Christmas that year, a hundred men went to work under a $56,000 WPA project. Their job was to build six tennis courts, a baseball diamond, and a golf course. They expected eight months work. The Legion contributed an additional $10,000, in memory of their war dead.

In 1940, Sears, Roebuck and Company provided funds for a community center in Legion Park. Nearly fifty years old, the building remains in the park today. The public coping with World War II needed to find their recreation close to home. During the summer of 1944, when pleasure driving was banned to save petroleum for the war effort, bus runs were added in Everett. Gasoline rationing combined with the growth in the north end of the city meant more visitors to the parks. When the soldiers came home in 1945, park use continued to grow like the reunited families.

Indians returned to the point in 1950. From 1950 to 1958, they were housed in a surplus World War II building. The thirty-some employees formed the Western Washington Agency of the federal bureau.

When the Everett School District needed a location for a junior college, the park board responded by donating 7.7 acres in 1951. The donation required voters' approval. Two years later, in October 1953, the city and school district agreed to terms. The deed was signed on July 6, 1954. That fall, in September 1954, two acres of land were leased to the Snohomish County Museum. The happy days of the '50s were heydays for club memberships. People were joiners, and a park like Legion was the perfect spot to get together.

The Sunset Garden club met at the park, as did the Men's Garden Club of Snohomish County, led by president A. M. Glassberg, editor of the *Everett Daily Herald* and the Everett Garden Club. In the winter of 1957, several huge trees were felled to allow picnic grounds and a rose garden. The Memory Rose Garden started that year by John Hall remains today at Legion Hall.

Wednesday nights saw the Everett Archery Club. And there was the Lawn Bowling Club. There was a fragrance garden for the blind. A Japanese garden to be known as the Everett Garden Club Roadside Park was approved by Mayor George Gebert in 1961, but never completed. A small arboretum was established on the northern edge of the golf course in 1963 and Cherry Tree Lane was added in 1976. In 1968, Eleanor Ballew sold three additional lots to the city. And that year, Everett Community College carpentry classes finished the picnic shelter. Facilities as diverse as a covered outdoor kitchen and the Snohomish County Museum have shared Legion's acreage.

In 1981, it was discovered that the park had never been formally dedicated. The city chose July 4 to rectify that oversight.

Today, Legion's 140 acres tell a story of early history on the point: the forest in the beginning, the Snohomish tribe, Blackman's Mill and millworkers, Depression funds, war rationing, and war heroes.

American Legion Memorial Golf Course

A public green rolls over 140 acres at American Legion Memorial Park. The vast majority is groomed for golf. The park itself uses just 11 acres of land here. The other 129 acres are dedicated to eighteen holes of play on the American Legion Memorial Golf Course.

This was the town's first public golf course. The only other course in Everett in the early years was the private membership Everett Golf and Country Club south of town. The land was part of the acreage acquired by the American Legion in 1932 for a park on Blackman's Point. The vision of the World War I veterans who made up Earl Faulkner Post No. 6 resulted in an impressive recreational complex. Their development of the park and golf course did much to develop the residential area around the park as well.

By the 1930s, the game of golf had moved beyond its early reputation as a game for the old or the rich. Still, there were only 343 golf courses in the entire country. Compare that

In 1954, the big news was the new stove at Legion Park. Over the years, many groups have held a variety of events in Legion Hall and the surrounding area.
Everett Herald

In 1974, the park board voted to form a Junior Golf Association. Today Everett School District's golf team practices on both Legion and Walter Hall Golf Courses.
Ray Watters, *Everett Herald*

Mayor George Gebert and three other City Officials check out Legion Hall's new kitchen. Mayor Gebert initiated many of Legion Park's improvements such as the Japanese Garden and the Arboretum on the northern edge of the Golf Course.
Ray Watters, photographer; Everett Herald

Bruce Wier, assistant pro at Legion Golf Course.

The Everett Parks Department and the General Hospital Foundation have been leading innovators in the "Health Companion" programs. The program allows medically at risk people to maintain radio communications with the Club House in case of an emergency.

Park Department maintenance crews are constantly working to keep Legion and Walter E. Hall Golf Courses in tip top shape.

to 1986, when there were more than 12,000 courses nationwide.

With Works Progress Administration funds and much of their own money, the local Legion post saw the golf course built. Then on October 2, 1935, they transferred the title for all the park land at Blackman's Point to the city, with the agreement that the Legion would continue to run the golf course. The Legion retained a little more than two acres to build a clubhouse and, on July 15, 1937, received a twenty-five-year lease from the city for the course. It was to be sooner than twenty-five years, however, that the city was back in the municipal golf course business.

A nine-hole golf course was opened on July 24, 1937. Jack Martin was the golf pro, and C. E. Pinkerton was his assistant and greenskeeper. The first foursome off the tee included Julian and George Rickles, Fred French, and Oscar Engelstead. That opening day Dr. A. H. Gunderson made the first eagle on the course, doing the long seventh hole in three. Verne Henry was said to have lost the first ball.

Play on eighteen holes of golf began in 1938. Some of the original nine holes were changed, and the finished product was a 6,128-yard, par seventy-three course laid out by Chandler Egan, one of the nation's top golfers at the time. Golf tournaments of every sort became regular events at Legion and often included cross play at the Everett Golf and Country Club and the Hillcrest Golf Club in Marysville, later renamed Cedarcrest.

By the early 1940s, the Legion post wanted out of the no-profit golf course business. The remainder of the Legion's lease on the course was canceled, and the city of Everett was in the municipal golf course business. The course that came to be known as "Muni" was reborn. As a recreational facility within the city, the renamed Everett Municipal Golf Course then came under the supervision of the parks department.

May 21, 1944, was opening day for the Snohomish County Amateur Golf Association Tournament, an institution since 1931. The tournament was tied to the dedication of the new municipal course and included picnic plans at the park and a concert.

A good-sized crowd came to hear Mayor Henry Arends and Arthur Cook, commander of the Earl Faulkner Post of the American Legion, rededicate the course. Thornton Sullivan, then-chairman of the park department, was master of ceremonies.

A new pro came on in July of 1944. Ray Glenzer moved from the assistant pro's job at Everett Golf and Country Club to the top job at Muni. He spent his first summer fulfilling a war recreational program by providing community youth and adult defense workers with free golf lessons.

Profits, or the lack of them, plagued the course again in the late 1940s and early 1950s. The course did not consistently make money, and some members of the park board were concerned about a drain on general park funds. The city agreed to underwrite the golf course losses and reimburse the park fund until the situation improved.

The most famous golfer of the day, President Dwight Eisenhower, was in the White House in 1953. Ike was doing his part to popularize the game. At the same time, Everett Junior College was negotiating for room to expand, and the southwest corner of the golf course fit their purposes to a tee.

And so it was that the original 15th hole met its demise when 7.7 acres of land for the new college campus were transferred from the city to the college district. Holes 13, 14, and 16 were also affected. No money exchanged hands, but the school district assumed the cost of altering and improving the landscape of the course.

The deed was signed on July 6, 1954. When work at the course was completed, the 16th hole was shortened from a par 5 to a par 4, and the golf course went from a par 73 to a par 72. In 1955, a junior college student named Bob Whisman hit the course record of 64 for eighteen holes. Whisman returned in 1965 as the pro at Legion. It's a job he holds today.

In October 1959, the park board proposed changing the course's name to acknowledge once again the Legion's involvement. The course became the American Legion Municipal Golf Course. In 1970, when the present clubhouse was built, the course was rededicated as American Legion Memorial Golf Course. The clubhouse sits on top of a hill today, moved up from its original location just off the road.

Over the years, whenever the course was changed, course records began anew. In 1989, the record stands at 62, scored by Jeff Knudson in the first round of the Monte Cristo Tournament in 1982.

"Probably the most outstanding thing about this course is the amount of play it gets today," Whisman said in summer 1989. "Years ago, we never had starting times. There just weren't that many golfers. The statistic going around today is that if you built a new golf course every day until the year 2000, you still wouldn't have enough courses to meet the need."

Golf Pro Bob Whisman at Legion and Walter E. Hall golf courses is in demand for golf lessons.

At Legion, it's a time of fine-tuning. In 1986 and 1987, drainage, irrigation, and cart paths were all improved, and a medical alert radio system was installed. You can gauge the age of the golfers by what they call the course. But whether golfers are playing at Legion or "Muni," the game's the same. And the memorial is still fitting, however it's remembered.

While their sons were fighting in the midst of World War II, the citizens of Everett were busy building tomorrows on the homefront. The park and golf course they began on Blackman's Point north of town was a beautiful vision that came true.

Kasch Memorial Park

"Play ball!" rings in the air at Kasch Memorial Park.

Much of this recently developed regional park was designed with Little League baseball teams and adult softball games in mind. Under construction are three tournament-sized soccer fields, a four-field softball complex, a caretaker space and office building, play and picnic areas, additional parking, and landscaping. Further plans are on the drawing boards.

It wasn't always so. This was land that belonged to the federal government and was used as a missile test site by the Air Force.

In the early 1970s, the government declared some two hundred acres here surplus. Sen. Henry M. Jackson used his know-how to get sixty acres for the city. The senator knew how to play ball himself. The General Services Administration signed the deed on the day after Christmas 1972.

It was during Everett Mayor Robert Anderson's term that this property referred to as the Paine Field Annex was acquired for park and recreational purposes. The land was needed to serve a rapidly growing population in the south of town.

Still, it took thirteen years to see the results of that day-after-Christmas gift. Although the city accepted the land from the federal government, they had no money at the time to develop the park. By the middle 1970s, the federal government threatened to reclaim the land if developments weren't forthcoming. To save the property, the city built inexpensive walking trails. But continued budget restraints and higher priorities kept the property largely undeveloped until the middle 1980s.

Voters turned down a $5 million bond issue in 1980 to develop the property. Citizens did

respond to the city's request for suggestions to name the park. At the time, the property was being informally referred to as Peace Park. A petition with more than a thousand signatures was received in favor of the late Bill Kasch. In June 1981, the park board voted to approve the suggestion. It was Bill Kasch who helped start Little League baseball in Everett. He was a volunteer with that organization for more than twenty-five years.

A star in his own right, Kasch earned sixteen letters in basketball, baseball, track, and football at Anacortes High School in the 1920s. Until the Depression forced him to drop out of college, he was working toward a teaching degree. Instead, he came to Everett in 1936 to work in Weyerhaeuser's new sulfite mill. Kasch worked his way up to become a shift superintendent and stayed to retire from the mill in 1974. His work with kids began in 1948 when he took on responsibilities as a basketball coach for Immaculate Conception School. He continued at that practice for twenty-seven years. Kasch also organized an adult Industrial Basketball League and played for the Weyerhaeuser team.

In 1953, Kasch was chosen by the *Everett Daily Herald* as the Man of the Year in Sports in recognition of his many volunteer activities. Born January 25, 1909, Kasch died November 24, 1980. In February 1983, Dick Rowley was also recognized for his volunteer work when the city council agreed to name the baseball complex at Kasch Park the Dick Rowley Memorial Complex.

With the continued growth in the south end of town, the city looked hard at new ways to develop the Kasch property. Phase I of Kasch Park was completed in spring 1985 at a cost of $451,000.

The park was dedicated on May 11, 1985. It opened with one regulation softball field and one senior Little League field, an entry road, parking, and restrooms. Underground wiring, drainage, and irrigation were put in place for future projects within the park.

Located at 8811 Airport Road across from Boeing, Kasch is a regional park of sixty acres. Besides the athletic facilities, there are planned walking areas and an environmentally sensitive area containing a bog.

This is a park in progress. Phase II development is under way. More matching funds were requested for three tournament-sized soccer fields. There will be four additional regulation softball fields of tournament caliber, complete with lights, bleachers, announcer's booth, and concession stand. The Snohomish County Council helped in February 1987 with a gift of $25,000

Mayor Bill Moore leads the way in groundbreaking ceremonies at Kasch Park. Facilities at the park include a new
cloverleaf softball complex and soccer fields.

for ball parks.

On the quiet side, a nature trail system will
circle the park for jogging or walking. Designed
to meander through the wooded areas surrounding the park, the trail will be located to
provide safe pedestrian access to facilities
throughout the park.

Picnic areas and children's play areas will
also be offered within the park. The wooded
area adjacent to the golf course is being discussed as an overnight camping area during
sports tournaments.

In 1988, the Everett City Council at Mayor Moore's request
voted to approve major park improvements. Included is
construction of three soccer fields and a tournament quality softball complex at Kasch Park. Construction for these
improvements began in the summer of 1989.

As the Lowell Booth at the County Fair shows, Lowell has always had a sense of community pride. This civic pride led residents to request the City Council build a park in Lowell. In 1966, groundbreaking began and Lowell Park remains one of Everett's popular neighborhood parks.

Chapter 6

Community and Regional Parks

Garfield Park
Lowell Park
Riverdale Park

Garfield Park

In 1915 the Lillian Stephens Women's Christian Temperance Union asked the city to establish a park in the Riverside area on Everett's east side. The women were picky enough to specify the square block between Chestnut and Walnut streets from Twenty-third to Twenty-fourth. The Riverside Commercial Club backed up the request, but it was two years before a park was created half a mile south. This later became Riverdale Park.

It wasn't until 1931 that the city bought the land designated by the WCTU, along with the block east of it. The new park was described as a "willow swamp" frequented by "willow goldfinches." The land bisects Chestnut Street, and motorists sometimes drove through the swamp rather than go around to the next street. Neighborhood children kept a supply of wood and rope hidden in nearby bushes. When a car became stuck in the swampy mud, they would help the driver extricate it—for a small fee.

In 1932 the federal Works Progress Administration accepted Garfield Park as one of its early projects. WPA crews took dirt from a high section on the east side of the park to fill the swampy midsection. They removed brush which, according to local legend, had provided cover for bootleggers' operations during prohibition. At about the same time the city posted signs prohibiting cattle grazing, apparently putting an end to yet another customary use of the land.

Early development included a small playground. As time passed, a small fieldhouse, called the Hobby House, was built at the corner of Twenty-fourth and Walnut. It was used for children's crafts, and in 1941 was the workshop that turned out five hundred Christmas presents. The building and other facilities were demolished when the park was renovated in the 1970s. By that time, the field was being used for both Little League and adult slow-pitch softball play. These games became so popular and the teams so numerous that the park was often booked from 8 a.m. until after midnight.

The congestion and noise of the games weren't welcome in the neighborhood. The community in late 1976 organized the Garfield Community Service League to work with the city on the neighborhood's parks. Together they worked out a plan to combine planning for Garfield and Riverdale under an open space park and recreation plan the city had developed in 1973. The adult leagues moved to Riverdale and the Little League groups developed a facility of their own at Garfield. The Garfield Community Service League merged with the Greater Riverside Organization in November 1980, and the larger group continued to work for improvements to the park until it featured two Little League fields, basketball hoops, a playground, tennis courts, horseshoes, picnic tables, and open space.

Garfield Park was cooperatively re-masterplanned to meet the needs of the Garfield neighborhood.

Garfield Park is a popular neighborhood park. A Works
Progress Administration Project, it was constructed in 1932.

A 1950s aerial view of the Lowell Paper Mill. The area on the left side of the Snohomish River became Everett's twenty-eighth park in 1989. This area is named Rotary Park.
Everett Public Library

Lowell Park

The Snohomish River swells as it rolls down its broad, flat valley until it reaches Ebey Island several miles above Puget Sound. There, where the river splits in two, E. D. Smith settled in 1863. Smith logged to build a lumber mill, a home, a store, a hotel, a post office, and a school. He prospered so greatly that at one time he had 150 employees. In 1872 he platted a town site that he called Lowell. The old mill town was annexed to Everett in 1962. Lowell citizens had decided to annex primarily because they wanted the city's water and sewer service. But they also wanted a park.

The Lowell Civic Group persuaded Simpson Lee Company and the Everett Improvement Company to donate land and then offered to turn it over to the park board in 1964. A newspaper contest gave the park its original name of Candy Cane Park. The civic group held weekend work parties to prepare the site, using bull-

dozers supplied by the city.

In July 1969, the city council asked for money from the state to develop several parks, including Candy Cane Park. A month later Mayor Robert Anderson attended the park board meeting to say there had been numerous protests about the park's name. It was changed to Lowell Community Park. It was June the next year when construction began on a ball field, wading pool, children's play area, sitting area, horseshoe pits, bicycle and foot paths, picnic area, and restrooms. The park was completed in 1972 and won a landscaping award from the Washington State Nurserymen's Association.

The community heard an unpleasant rumor about its park in 1980—that it would soon be neighbors with a diesel repair facility. The civic group asked the city to use federal funds to buy the property. The land brought the park to four acres, and the park board built tennis courts in the new area. During the 1980s the wading pool was abandoned and replaced with a large picnic shelter.

*E. D. Smith, shown with his family, was the founder of Low-
ell. The Snohomish River site where Smith built his mill is
now the location of Rotary Park.*
Everett Public Library

*Situated on the Snohomish River, Lowell Park was com-
pleted in 1972 and was originally Candy Cane Park.*

Riverdale Park

The Snohomish River flows quietly beside Everett's eastern border until it veers left into Puget Sound, forming the peninsula where the city was built. In ages past the swirling water carved a gently sloping shoulder near where that left turn begins. With a little judicious earth-moving, the slope was destined to become a fine park with play areas, open space and, above all, baseball diamonds.

The land was bought from the Everett Improvement Company in March 1917 for $10,000. Park board member Jacob Anthes and City Commissioner T. J. Kelly donated $5 each as the prize for a name-the-park contest. The winner was six-year-old Charles Dana True, who suggested Riverdale. The *Everett Herald* said at the time that the board chose the name because: "In the first place it locates the pleasure ground as being on the river; the second value is its restful and poetic sound."

Bonds approved by the voters in 1919 were sold in March 1922, and the park board authorized park Superintendent Oden Hall to plant the first seeds of Riverdale Park. Two years later, the *Everett News* reported: "A small army of carpenters will set to with hammer and saw on the work of building a modern community house for auto campers." The structure had a roofed area walled in on one end to provide for restrooms. The other sides were open and had eight picnic tables, benches, a community stove, and running water.

The tourist camp operated until 1928, but plans to develop the park in new ways were derailed by the Depression. Then, in 1938, Riverdale was chosen for a Works Progress Administration project—a baseball diamond.

The plans apparently hit a snag in 1939, possibly because the city was involved in transactions that netted 2.4 acres of additional land for the park. By the end of April 1940, WPA workers were completing the development of a four-acre baseball diamond. The infield and outfield were grassed, drain fields were in place, and 2,040 feet of pipe had been installed for a sprinkling system. A water department office building was being rebuilt as a fieldhouse with shower rooms for the players.

The schedule for dedication ceremonies on May 12, 1940, included appearances by Everett officials, the mayors of all the cities in Snohomish County, and state WPA Administrator Carl Smith. Coach Jim Ennis introduced the players of the Pilchucks, the city's newly organized Northwest League baseball team. The team played its first home game at the end of the ceremonies. Nearly two thousand spectators watched the home team lose 2-1 to the Bremerton Cruisers in extra innings.

The park continued as a community baseball center for many years. It also was the site for at least one appearance of the "donkey baseball" troupe that had been a feature at the Chicago World's Fair in 1932. The Riverdale performance, in 1943, was sponsored by local businesses and civic organizations, some of which provided the riders who mounted the donkeys for games of softball, polo, and a donkey rodeo. By 1957 the Riverdale Park diamond was the home field for the Everett Babe Ruth League and for the Everett Bluejays and Paine Air Force Base teams of the Cascade League.

In 1977 the city park director Chuck Logan and park staff prepared a master development plan for Garfield and Riverdale parks in cooperation with the neighborhoods. Riverdale was rebuilt to provide the 16.77-acre park with a fitness court, restrooms, two softball fields, a playground, and a large, grassy open space. In 1988 the park board was considering plans to add a new softball complex and a picnic area.

Local visitors to Riverdale Park enjoying a warm summer day.

Land for Riverdale Park was purchased in 1917. Today, the park is home to two softball fields, a playground and a fitness court donated by General Hospital Foundation.

Local baseball players enjoy a quiet practice game at Riverdale Ballpark in April 1954. The park was built by the Works Progress Administration during the 1930s.
Everett Herald

The U.S. Olympic Women's Rowing Team held daily work-outs at Langus Riverfront Park on the Snohomish River during the summer of 1988 in preparation for the Seoul Olympic Games.

Chapter 7

Scenic View Parks

Harborview Park
Langus Riverfront Park
North and
South View Parks
Rotary Parks

Harborview Park

It's an eyeful of mountains and sunsets, expansive bay and working waterfront. It's the telescopic view of a city far enough distant to look perfect. A visit to Harborview Park begins with a straightforward look at the here and now. But the view may lead to speculation about the past and the future. It's a place to wonder how small the canoes of the Snohomish tribe must have seemed in these waters, about the uncharted beauty that Captain Vancouver must have found, about how a city of stumps changes to support these thousands of people in the space of little more than a hundred years.

Harborview Park on Mukilteo Boulevard is a place to get a perspective on things. Jacob and David Livingston were here 127 years ago. Theirs was the site of the first steam-powered sawmill in Snohomish County. Thirty years before Everett was incorporated, they built their mill in 1863. Nine years later, the Livingstons attempted to further develop the property. Their plat of "Western New York" was the first property

Harborview Park is a popular spot to view the spectacular view of Puget Sound.

platted on Port Gardner Bay.

Now the old Livingston property lies just inside the city limits of Everett on the road to Mukilteo. For years, people crossed the railroad tracks here to make their way to the beach. Previously known as the Great Northern view site, Harborview is one of several Everett parks on leased land. The park's two and a half acres sit above the tracks and are part of the railroad right of way.

The lease was entered into with the Great Northern Railroad Company on May 25, 1964. The price was $5 a year. In May 1983, the lease was increased to $180 per year, now with Burlington Northern Railroad. It continues on an annual renewal. The Everett Garden Club donated more than 150 hours of work on cleanup and landscaping. As part of the lease agreement with the railroad, the city agreed to build a fence along the western boundary to discourage people from crossing the tracks. Total cost of the project, including work and donations by the garden club, the Great Northern, and the parks department, was $4,875.

Picnic tables were added and the park was completed and named by the park board in July 1967. Restrooms were approved in May 1972 and later removed due to vandalism. The parking lot was completed in August 1973.

There is no longer beach access. There is a large parking area close to the road where the view alone pulls in travelers on Mukilteo Boulevard. The Everett Jetty and Hat Island are full ahead in Port Gardner Bay. The Tulalip Reservation and Camano Island lie across the bay to the north and west. Visitors to Harborview can see clear to Weyerhaeuser's mill on the Snohomish River and pick out its smoke stack. North Everett bends around Port Gardner Bay and the Port of Everett stretches around the bend giving berth to merchant ships from around the world. Navy ships docked in Port Gardner Bay in World War II, and are expected again with the completion of the proposed Navy Homeport.

Parks provide an interesting perspective on what a city chooses to preserve for its citizens. At Harborview, there is an enormous sense of place. Visitors look in three directions. They can also look backward and forward, at Everett's past, and its future.

Harborview Park doesn't just offer something to look at. It offers something to think about.

Harborview Park is a popular spot to watch the sailboats and ferries on Puget Sound.

View of Puget Sound from Harborview Park.

Langus Riverfront Park

The Snohomish River and Union Slough backwaters join to create Smith Island at the northern edge of Everett. The island has a history of being cut off from the mainland and largely ignored, while the river it edges has seen most of the activity. The Snohomish tribe paddled cedar canoes in this waterway. Traders and trappers took a turn. Early settlers of the Washington Territory, including physician Henry A. Smith, diked the shoreline at Smith Island to allow farming. At the turn of the century, mills grew up across the river's banks and business was furious for a time. When the timber was gone and the mills followed, nature began the slow process of reclaiming the Snohomish River.

The State Department of Natural Resources developed boat launches and a camping area for twentieth century people on the southwest shore of Smith Island, then largely abandoned them for lack of funding. A portion of the land was used for storing sand dredged from the river. Isolated, the Smith Island launching area became a dumping ground. Alongside fish and wildflowers were abandoned car bodies and rusted appliances. The sounds of nature were drowned by the noise of off-road vehicles climbing the sand pile. The river was no longer the main arterial. The lanes of Interstate 5 ran through the island, with Burlington Northern tracks just across the river to the south.

Both plagued and blessed by the waters that surround it, Smith Island had seen better days. About half of the two thousand-acre island was annexed by Everett in 1983, including the old boat launch and the huge sand pile.

As the surrounding area became more urban, Everett rediscovered the river's potential. A regional park was planned on a mile-long strip of land. It would be called Langus Riverfront Park, to honor a veteran city council member who had taken a lifelong interest in the city's parks. Volunteers helped give the new park project its boost. More than sixty people showed up one April day in 1987 to help city park employees begin the clean-up. They removed thirteen tons of garbage. Mayor Bill Moore and the city council officially moved to preserve the place. The project was part of the city's $25 million Capital Improvement Program set in motion in December 1987 to fund recreation and culture.

Langus Riverfront Park at Smith Island, the city's first riverfront park, was dedicated and officially opened on September 7, 1988. Mayor Moore said the city couldn't have chosen a better namesake than William J. Langus, the city's longest-serving council member. He was a member of the original Freeholders Committee, which established the city charter. He was elected to council in 1968 as part of the city's changeover to a charter form of government. Bill Langus helped found the Everett Boys Club, served for years on the Everett School Board, and pushed for park development in the city. He wasn't the only one who had a good time at the dedication ceremonies. Festivities included boat tours on the *Snohomish River Queen,* a Woman's U.S. Olympic Rowing Team and Everett Rowing team contest, a balloon launch, children's games, and music.

There's much to enjoy at the park. A two-lane public boat launch puts power boats in the Snohomish. The fishing pier and floating dock move sports enthusiasts nearer to the water. At the south end of the parking lot is a low dock for rowing shells and kayaks. There are picnic tables, a meeting room, a paved parking lot, and restrooms.

At the park site, the river glides around the tiny Ferry Baker Islands midstream. Three miles downstream boaters meet Port Gardner Bay. Ten miles upstream is the town of Snohomish. The park makes a perfect location for a canoe, kayak, or boat trip up the river to explore the beautiful Snohomish Estuary. The Everett Rowing Association finds the river a popular place for rowers because it is protected from wind and uncongested.

On shore, Langus Riverfront Park is perfect for bird watching. Bordering on wetlands, a river walkway and interpretive trails bring visitors close to wildlife.

Work on the park continues. A caretaker's residence, play equipment, a nature interpretive center, public art, and a four-mile pedestrian/bicycle path are in the works. The park is built with people in mind. The river it edges is in the mainstream of activity again, bending with the times.

Hundreds of people turned out at the dedication of Langus Riverfront Park to honor Councilman Bill Langus.

Langus Riverfront Park is a popular fishing spot with the local Salmon and Steelheaders Club.

North and South View Parks

The travelers on West Marine View Drive who pull off the road to enjoy the bay view probably don't know they're in one of Everett's parks. The only signs here were made by nature.

North and South View Parks are twin pockets of pleasure on a road designed to showcase Everett's waterfront. Together they add just 4.5 acres to the city's parkland, but size is no measure of their impact. North View Park sits next to door manufacturer Nord Door of Everett. South Park is just a jog away from Tenth Street and the entrance to the public boat launch. The parks were formed when the city widened Norton Avenue and changed its name to create West Marine View Drive. The project left the remaining land on the water too small for development.

South View Park's land was bought from American Tugboat Company for $1. A few months later, on January 20, 1974, North View Park was purchased from the Scott Paper Company for $5,529. Two parking areas provide pull-off places to enjoy the beauty of Port Gardner Bay. A wide walkway connects the two parks. Benches are planted near beds of wild roses and flowering groundcover, and a long row of poplar breaks the wind. For travelers without time to stop, the parks offer a stretch of tended landscape along West Marine View Drive.

Mornings, the gulls swoop in for breakfast. At tide change, birds track the mud with their wanderings. At sunset, a golden orange sky puts a glow on log booms in the bay. The panorama changes with the time and the tide. And there's another kind of beauty here. Logs ready for shipment around the world wait here, buoyed at high tide, scattered in the sand at low tide. You're looking at Everett's beginnings and a vital part of today's economy.

Named by Everett Parks Department employees as a simple means of identification, North and South View Parks are more beautiful than their names suggest.

Rotary Park

When Dennis Brigham settled on the peninsula at the foot of the Snohomish River around 1861, he was pretty much alone. But only two short years later, E. D. Smith arrived on the other side of the peninsula and started a logging operation where the river splits to form Ebey Island. He cut the huge, virgin timber beside the river,

then floated the logs downstream to the quiet backwaters of a sharp bend in the river. It was at this bend that he built his lumber mill and founded the Lowell community.

More than a century later, Everett Mayor Bill Moore set out to strengthen the city's recreational and cultural facilities and in turn improve the quality of life for future residents. Moore, the city council, and city departments established Kasch and Langus Riverfront parks, scheduled plans for a new library and civic center, and worked to improve existing facilities.

Then in 1985, the owners of fifty-nine acres along the Lowell River Road just east of the city limits annexed their property to the city. Moore, who had lived in Lowell for a time when he was a boy, moved with the city council to accept the annexation and quickly arranged a land trade with the Simpson Lee Company for 1.5 acres. That gave the city ownership of a former boat launch site which they quickly moved to reopen. The city also moved to install improvements and initiate a strict patrol to reduce vandalism in the area.

Then city officials, with the aid of the State Interagency Committee for Outdoor Recreation, purchased an adjacent eleven acres for $118,000 from the Maltby Tank and Barge Company. That acquisition included the site of E. D. Smith's original lumber mill.

About the same time the Everett Rotary Club donated $50,000 to the city to help develop a pedestrian trail along the riverfront. Club members and Lowell residents held a work party on the site during the spring of 1989 and collected many tons of refuse which had accumulated over the decades. On March 22, 1989, the city council officially named the area Rotary Park in recognition of the club's help in financing and preparing the land.

The new park was maintained largely in its natural state during its early days. Smith's mill had long since been demolished and, aside from a few old pilings along the river bank, there was little sign that there ever had been major development there.

Then the city approached county officials with a proposal to jointly develop the park so that it would include county owned land just outside the city limits. County Executive Willis Tucker and Councilwoman Liz McLaughlin agreed and presented a check to Mayor Bill Moore for $25,000. Preliminary plans call for the park's entry where Smith's mill used to be located. The Rotary Club's pedestrian trail will follow closely along the riverbank and will parallel a nature trail. The boat launch will bisect

the park and is served with an enlarged parking area and restrooms. Wetlands, just east of the boat launch, are accessible by a boardwalk. The plans also show a picnic area and a riverfront viewpoint.

Langus Riverfront Park was named after Councilman Bill Langus in September 1988. The city's longest-serving council member, he helped found the Everett Boys Club and has long been a supporter of park projects.

The future for Everett Parks brings a special challenge. Restoration and expansion are planned to meet the recreational needs of Everett. Mayor Bill Moore and Park Director Bob Cooper review plans for future park development on the Snohomish River.

Everett Parks Today and Tomorrow

The history of Everett parks is a story of thoughtful process and occasional expediency. It is the story of how more than seven hundred acres of park land were preserved over the years by a population that could not possibly have foreseen the future need. For ours is a place that has changed from a city of stumps and smokestacks to an aerospace giant and high-tech corridor in less than a hundred years.

From the first acquisitions of Clark and Forest parks in 1894, past generations made a commitment to preserve recreational land for the people of Everett. Sure, they did it for themselves, but they did it for us, too.

As the city of Everett grows and changes to meet the twenty-first century, so the park system will evolve. The need for outdoor fitness courts, spiral slides, or soccer fields was unknown when Clark and Forest parks were developed at the turn of the century. Folks wanted a place to congregate on a Sunday afternoon, maybe play a game of ball or ride a swing. They wanted a grassy hill preserved for them to spread a picnic blanket or walk hand-in-hand with a child.

When Everett was young and uncrowded, children played in fields of stumps and along the banks of the river. That is no longer possible. Now they need to be assured of neighborhood parks and an unspoiled beach.

Environmental issues were not a consideration in those early days. They are often our first concern today. The wetlands at Langus Riverfront, the bog at Kasch Park, Pigeon Creek at Forest Park, the eroding bank at Grand Avenue Park are all cause for our attention.

For the future, much is in the wind.

Port Gardner Bay looks forward. We are soon to be home to a Navy aircraft fleet. The Port greets merchant ships from around the world. Recreational boats fill our marina. Our shingle mills are long gone and the wood products industry is changing.

Highly technical computer and electronics businesses are booming.

New people are coming to Everett. And what of the people?

An Arborist for the Everett Parks Department, Dave Wilson keeps busy planting, transplanting, pruning, spraying, and fertilizing over six thousand trees around Everett.

Recreation Leader John Covert teaches a group of children how to be safe in the water.

One of the primary goals of the parks department is to "protect, preserve, and enhance parks, open spaces, and waterfront for the people." Maintenance and rehabilitation of our current parks, land and waterfront acquisition, and the people and equipment to accomplish those responsibilities, are central to the success of the parks department in the 1990s.

Look for the city to acquire more waterfront property and pursue the development of Jetty Island with the Port of Everett. Watch for additional softball, baseball, and soccer fields and the continued development of parks to meet the needs of South Everett.

We citizens of Everett today live in a place very different from the early pioneers. The need for a quiet and beautiful corner in a crowded world is more important than ever. Because those who have come before us created such a varied park system, some of the most prized land in the city is preserved for us. When visitors take in the view from Grand Avenue Park, American Legion Memorial Park, or North and South View Parks, they look to our past—and our future.

Now, as then, the need to provide and protect park land for tomorrow is vital, for who can imagine how citizens will use—and need—their parks a hundred years from now.

Matt Romanelli, a Landscaper in the Horticulture Division of the Parks Department prepares soil in one of the planter boxes at City Hall.

Peewee Picassos practice their techniques in one of the many recreation classes especially for children.

From 1894 to 1989, Everett has grown from a milltown to a modern city with a park system we can all be proud of. Park Architect Theo Mittet and assistant Cindi Pedersen review plans for development of soccer and softball fields at Kasch Park funded in December of 1987 by the Everett City Council.

Mowing over two hundred acres of grass is a major job for the maintenance crews at the Everett Parks Department, but it's all in a day's work for Pat Mattern.

Behind the scenes, the Everett Parks Department participates in many activities that are not park oriented such as helping to organize the dedication for Everett's Viet Nam Memorial.

Kids in Parks (KIP) is an award-winning program created to educate elementary school children about their parks. KIP develops an understanding about the value of parks and the environment through discussion, park visits, and environmental projects.

Horticulturalist Geoff Larsen and his staff are responsible for the hanging baskets and flowerbeds that beautify Everett each spring and summer.

Volunteers are an important part of the Parks Department donating over twenty thousand hours each year.

Everett has a rich and valuable resource in our 750 acres of park lands. More than 28 parks are available for leisure and recreational pursuits with opportunities for everyone.

Park Maintenance Superintendent Harold Shaw reviews plans with his staff for the development of future parks projects.

Working with the Private Industry Council (PIC) and Employment Security, Everett Parks and Recreation provides summer employment to low income youths between the ages of fourteen and twenty-one. PIC youth crews assist the Horticulture Division by doing landscaping work at the entries to Forest Park and along Mukilteo Boulevard.

Athletic Field Supervisor Bob Springer coordinates the maintenance and preparation of eighteen athletic fields. This includes caring for the turf, lining the fields, leveling ground, maintaining the bases and mounds, and irrigating the fields.

Youth Gymnastics, a class offered by the Parks Department, teaches children coordination and balance as they learn routines on the balance beam, parallel bars, vault, and floor.

The Everett Youth Basketball program's success is directly linked to the participation of volunteer coaches. These men and women provide leadership and act as positive role models donating hundreds of hours to help young people learn about the importance of teamwork.

League sports are offered year-round for both youths and adults. Over four thousand participate in rowing, soccer, softball, baseball, and basketball.

Education plays an important role in continuing the legacy of quality parks. Nature and interpretive walks, like the one these children are participating in, are a part of the education process.
Everett Parks and Recreation

Throughout the year, the Parks Department plays an important role in the success of local festivals, parades, and special events. Committed to the importance of community pride and tourism, park staff work behind the scenes to ensure that Art in the Park, Salty Sea Days, and the Fourth of July have the support they need to run quality events.

Within the park system there are miles of water pipes, irrigation lines, drainage lines, asphalt pathways, roadways, and electrical and communication lines that Park Maintenance crews have to keep in working order. Doug Ammons is doing just that as he checks pipes in the mechanical room at the Forest Park swim center.

Juanita Meyers, Instructor Mike Van Winkle, Marsh Sexton, and Jennifer Dupler participate in the Landscape Construction Class, a cooperative effort between the Everett School District and Everett Parks for Special Education students.

Internationally recognized, Everett's Adopt-A-Stream Program is an innovative program for stream rehabilitation and salmon rearing.

Jim Shields, Assistant Director and Susan Francisco, Administrative Assistant select photographs for the Park history book.

Senior woodcarvers help to construct signs for Everett's
parks.

Gary Anderson, a maintenance mechanic for the Everett
Parks Department, welds together a handrail at Forest Park.

Park Rangers play an important part in educating Everett citizens about the importance of their environment.

A sunny day on the beach at Howarth Park.

Jetty Island offers people a variety of recreational opportunities including the chance to watch a spectacular sunset.

Everett's public boat launch offers people access to a variety of locations along Port Gardner Bay.

Over seven hundred hanging baskets filled with petunias, geraniums, impatiens, calceolaria, and lobelia grown in the Forest Park greenhouses beautify Everett every spring and summer.

Everett School District Horticulture student at work in Forest Park greenhouse.

Kids in Parks (KIP) is an award winning program in coopera-tion with the Everett School District teaching Everett's chil-dren the value of their parks.

Flower beds like this one at Grand Park, are planted and maintained by the Parks Department throughout the City.

A quiet moment on the Snohomish River.

Sailboards, rowboats, canoes and sailboats are available for rental at Silver Lake Park.

Autumn in Forest Park.

Athletes, adorned in the Silver Lake Triathlon's green swim caps, take time to adjust to the chilly water before swimming a mile around the lake.

The Gene Nastri School of Music is a cultural program for youth, co-sponsored by the Everett Parks and Recreation Department.

In its eighth year, Music in the Parks is a free popular summer program providing concerts in various parks and the downtown business district.

Art in the Park, sponsored by the Everett Cultural Commission, is a popular annual event which introduces the public to various art mediums, music, dance, and theater.

Salty Sea Days, Everett's annual summer festival.

Young juggler at the Everett Cultural Commission's Art in the Park in Forest Park.

Best friends at Camp Patterson, a special program for special people, in Silver Lake Park.

Camp Patterson at Silver Lake is a unique summer program for developmentally disabled children. Named after Police

Chief Frank Patterson, the day camp began in 1948 as a program for the city's school safety patrol.

Whirling fun at Forest Park.

Everett Youth Basketball offers youth the opportunity to learn the sport of basketball in a mildly competitive atmosphere.

Summer worker beautifies Everett.

Children enrolled in the recreation program Pooh and Friends Preschool at Forest Park participate in a variety of fun and educational activities.

The Animal Farm in Forest Park is a popular summer attraction for Everett area children and adults.

Kiwanis Park was totally renovated in 1989. New play
equipment, flowerbeds, grass, and pathways were some of
the improvements.

The Swim Center at Forest Park is visited by thousands of children and adults each year.

Tee time at Legion Memorial Golf Course.

Everett School District's High School rowers compete in a regatta at Langus Riverfront Park.

A snowy winter day in Forest Park.

1989 Parks and Recreation Staff.

With careful planning, the Parks Department can continue the legacy that early pioneers like Rockefeller and Friday brought to our community.

The Parks Department takes great pride in planting beautiful flowers each spring and summer throughout Everett.

Maintenance employees Jim Marriott, Gary Anderson, and Greg Bell make adjustments in the circulating and heating system for the Forest Park Swim Center.

Park and Golf Superintendent Hank Bowman and Supervisor Glen Sayles inspect hydraulic lines on a new tractor. Park and Golf staff are responsible for the maintenance and upkeep of over eight hundred acres of parkland, two public golf courses, Everett's street tree program, all public right-of-ways and Everett's beautification program through the hanging flower baskets and flowerbeds.

The late Sen. Henry "Scoop" M. Jackson and Everett Mayor Bill Moore attend a formal dinner in 1980. The Jackson family home overlooks Grand Avenue Park.

131

Children of all ages enjoy the Animal Farm at Forest Park.

The Forest Park Animal Farm is a popular destination for residents and visitors to Everett.

Everett City Council

*Connie Niva,
President*

*Bill Langus,
Vice-President*

Dr. Ed Diamond

Carl Gipson

Ed Morrow

Dale Pope

Bob Overstreet

Everett Park Board

Arlene Diamond,
Chairperson

Ross Hoagland,
Vice-Chairperson

Gordon Hall

Don Hopkins

Dave Deveney

Dr. Don Barbacovi

Dr. Arthur Grossman

The Everett Parks and Recreation Department would like to acknowledge past Park Board members who have served since the inception of the new City Charter for their generous support and valuable contributions to Everett:

Dona Anderson
Hans Anderson
Judy Baker
Margaret Benson-Lamus
Tom Borgford
Steve Chase
Ruth Clement
Bill Deller
Don Gilcrest

Ben Hansen
Marcia Keister
Rosalie Kosher
Jack Krause
John Lachner
Charles Lawrence
Ralph Mackey
Everett McGee
Stacy Millar

Everett Miller
Phil Rifner
Shirley Schapler
Eldon Schalka
Earl Whitt
Robyn Wicklund
Bob Wilson

135

Chronological History

1792: On June 4, Captain George Vancouver landed on the beach below what is today Grand Avenue Park.

1890: The Rucker brothers acquired the original Dennis Brigham Homestead with the exception of two acres which Brigham had contractually retained until his death. Over the next eighty years, those two acres were lost in a land shuffle of questionable ownership until Maggie Lamus of the Everett Parks and Recreation Board encouraged the City to acquire the land for a new park. The land is known today as Maggies Park.

1891: C. A. Blackman built his shingle mill. Today the point overlooking the original site is part of Legion Park, but for years was simply known as Blackman's Point.

1893: Everett was incorporated and became a certified city.

1893: Everett was severely crippled by the depression of 1893.

1893: During the depression, James J. Hill, known as the Empire Builder and owner of the Great Northern Railroad, came to Everett and bought out Rockefeller and other eastern investors.

1894: September 26, the block which is now known as Clark Park was purchased from the Everett Land Company for $21,535. This became the City's first park.

1894: On September 27, City Park was established. In 1931, City Park was renamed Clark Park.

1894: September 27, the first ten acres of Forest Park were purchased for $4,300 with the provision that $600 worth of improvements be done in the next five years.

1906: March 26, Grand Avenue Park was given to the City by the Everett Improvement Company.

1907: November 26, voters passed a new First Class City Charter which approved a five-man Park Commission to be appointed by the Mayor.

1909: Eighty acres of land were purchased from the Swalwell Land, Loan, and Trust Company to expand Forest Park.

1912: April 16, voters accepted new City Charter based on the Commission system. Charter changes Park Commission to a council appointed body of six members, one per councilman.

1913: Forest Park was officially named.

1914: The City of Everett acquired three deer, two coyotes, two pelicans, and monkeys, beginning the Forest Park Zoo.

1915: $2,000 was taken from the Park Budget to create an emergency fund putting unemployed to work on Forest Park improvements.

1916: Another section of land was purchased to expand Forest Park.

1916: The infamous Everett Massacre erupted between the mill owners and the Industrial Workers of the World.

1917: Riverdale Park was purchased from the Everett Improvement Company for $10,000. The school children of Riverside named the park.

1919: The Forest Park Zoo was officially established.

1919: November 19, voters passed a $50,000 bond issue providing funds for: purchase of Silver Lake; $10,000 in improvements to Riverdale Park; $13,000 for zoo, playground, and other Forest Park improvements; $20,000 for a bandstand and other improvements to Clark Park. Total assessed value of park land was placed at $61,756.

1920: Oden Hall was appointed assistant to H. W. North, the park superintendent.

1921: Oden Hall was appointed park superintendent.

1922: Land located on the fresh water shores of Silver Lake was purchased by the City of Everett from the Thomas Wilson Land Company.

1927: Maple Heights Bathing Beach was acquired.

1929: Small section of Forest Park (presently occupied by Floral Hall, the greenhouses, and the Administration Offices) was acquired from the Norwegian Luthern Church.

1930's: Forest Park, Clark Park, Riverdale Park, and Legion Park saw development under the workmanship of the Works Progress Administration.

1930's: In the 1930s Edgewater Park was developed by the Edgewater Playfield Association. The land was donated by Art Sorenson and Leo Loken.

1931: July 18, Garfield Park was deeded to the Park Department by the Everett Playground Association.

1931: City Park was renamed Clark Park after John C. Clark. Clark was one of the City's founding powers.

1932: February 15, the first section of Legion Memorial Park was given to the City as a gift from A. B. and Harriet Clausen.

1932: April, a wading pool was built at Forest Park through the efforts of the Everett Lions Club.

1932: The American Legion, Earl Falkner Post No. 6, donated land to the City of Everett. Land was also a gift to the City by the Everett Improvement Company and J. L. Rucker.

1933: Two ballfields were constructed at Garfield Park.

1937: On July 15, Walter E. Hall was named assistant superintendent to his brother Oden.

1937: July 24, the first foursome of Julian and George Rickles, Fred French and Oscar Englstead tee off at Legion Golf Course.

1939: Floral Hall was built through the Work Progress Administration (WPA) established by President Franklin Roosevelt.

1940: The construction of Floral Hall at Forest Park was completed.

1940: March 7, Park Board approved plans to install bleachers, grandstand and lights in Riverdale Park.

1940: The City acquired property at Thirty-sixth and Rockefeller. This property was later developed into Kiwanis Park.

1940: Sears and Roebuck donated the materials and funds to build a community center at Legion Park.

1940: On May 12, Riverdale Park was dedicated. The dedication coincided with the first ballgame held at Riverdale Stadium.

1941: November 5, the construction of a Community House at Legion Park began.

1941: In September, the City of Everett leased the Maple Heights Park in lower Forest Park to the Boy Scouts who used the Heights until 1948.

1941: The Army Air Corps leased Silver Lake Park as a recreation area for the troops at Paine Field. The lease expired in 1946.

1943: April 27, Edgewater Park was added to the Park System.

1943: Over $2,500 expended on Pigeon Creek #2 Bathing Beach which opened on July 1. The old Maple Heights Beach was abandoned and the overhead crossing was torn down.

1945: Alvin Weiss was appointed zookeeper.

1948: On January 9, John Hall, Walter E. Hall's son was hired by the Parks Department as a gardener.

1949: Frank Patterson started youth programs at Silver Lake Park.

1950: The Everett Development Company dedicated an 0.8 acre lot to the property owners in View Ridge for park purposes.

1951: The first school patrol camp at Silver Lake under Officer Frank Patterson took place.

1951: July 18, Ada and William Pilz donated 1.5 acres to the Everett School District. The acreage later was developed into Doyle Park.

1953: In July, John Hall was appointed assistant superintendent in charge of Legion Park.

1954: May 12, Rucker Hill Park was donated by Ruby and Jasper Rucker and Margaret Rucker-Armstrong.

1955: The Bridle Park Addition in Southwest Everett was platted in 1955. Pope A. Talbot, Inc., deeded a piece of land then to the property owner to be used for recreation.

1956: On May 10, John Hall replaced his father, Walter E. Hall, as Park Superintendent. John held the position until he retired on February 1, 1972.

1959: The View Ridge Community Club and the City of Everett reached a working agreement that left View Ridge Park's title with the VRCC and the maintenance duties with the Everett Parks Department.

1961: The Park Board named "Silver Lake," Thornton A. Sullivan Recreation Area, after a former board president.

1962: Most of the Forest Park Zoo was torn down due to monetary costs. The public had turned down three bond issues during the 1950s that would have allowed the zoo to survive.

1963: The Everett Community College Carpentry Class built a concession building at Forest Park. In 1973, the concession building became the Recreation Office.

1963: August, Camp Patterson, a day camp for the disabled was dedicated in honor of Mr. Frank Patterson for his hard work in rehabilitating the Silver Lake Beach.

1964: February 28, the Simpson Lee Company and the Everett Improvement Company donated Candy Cane Park (Lowell Park) to the City of Everett.

1964: The Edgewater Playfield Association donated their park to the City of Everett.

1965: The Everett Community College Carpentry Class built a picnic shelter on the northeast corner of the Kiddie Korral in Forest Park.

1967: The Parks and Recreation Department headquarters were moved out of City Hall and into the current Park Office at Forest Park. The Park Office was built by the Everett Community College Carpentry class.

1967: August 14, through an agreement developed between Great Northern Railroad Company and Park Superintendent, John Hall, the land known as Harborview Park was leased annually from the railroad.

1967: A Bond Issue was passed and $100,000 was approved for construction of Walter E. Hall Golf Course.

1968: February 28, Wiggums Hollow Park was acquired through the cooperative efforts of the parents in the Housing Project, the Community Action Council, the Inter-Church Committee for Social Action.

1970: Marked the creation of the Animal Farm at Forest Park.

1971: Howarth Park construction began.

1971: On October 20, Mayor Bob Anderson presided over a picnic dedication for Howarth Park.

1971: The City Council officially adopted the name Kiwanis Park.

1971: Judd and Black Park was built by the State of Washington and in March given to the City of Everett to maintain.

1972: The land for Kasch Park was acquired from the Heritage Conservation and Recreation Services.

1972: February 1, John Hall retired as Park Superintendent.

1972: On May 27, Mayor Bob Anderson held the dedication of Walter E. Hall Park in honor of former Superintendent, Walter E. Hall.

1972: Lowell Park won a landscaping award from the Washington State Nurserymen's Association.

1973: September 18, Lions Park was acquired with funds from the Land and Water Conservation Fund of the Bureau of Outdoor Recreation.

1974: Railroad overpass at Lower Howarth Park was constructed.

1974: The land for South View Park on Marine View Drive was purchased from the American Tugboat Company for $1.00.

1974: The land for North View Park on Marine View Drive was purchased from Scott Paper Company for $5,529.

1974: Howarth Park Trestle, over the railroad tracks, was completed.

1975: June 11, Lions Park officially opened to the public.

1975: Forest Park Swim Center opened to the public with a removable roof which was replaced with a permanent roof in 1985.

1975: Burlington Northern exchanged parcels of land with the City of Everett. This land became J. J. Hill Park in 1976.

1976: The Central Lions Club helped develop the J. J. Hill Park.

1978: The Silver Lake Kiwanis Club donated 0.6 acres to the City of Everett. The land was then added to the existing Silver Lake Park property.

1980: Wiggums Hollow was rejuvenated to its present state through a $5,000 grant made possible by the Everett Housing Authority.

1981: In June, the Park Board voted on the name of Kasch Memorial Park for their newest park.

1981: American Legion Memorial Park was officially dedicated.

1981: The City of Everett gave the Everett School District the western half of Clark Park. The School District then built six tennis courts for use by Everett High School and the public.

1981: In October, Dean and Carol Richardson donated 0.17 acres to the City of Everett. The land subsequently was added to the Silver Lake Park Area.

1983: Ballfield development began at Kasch Park.

1983: September, Snohomish County transferred the Wiggums Hollow Park to the City of Everett.

1983: About half of the two thousand acres of Smith Island land was annexed by Everett. 58 acres became Langus Riverfront Park in 1988.

1984: The School District offered the City of Everett a ten year lease for $1.00 a year in exchange for maintenance and upkeep of Doyle Park.

1984: Thanksgiving Day storm severely damaged Swim Center roof.

1985: May 11, Kasch Park was officially dedicated in honor of Bill Kasch.

1985: Lions Hall was built through a donation from the North Everett Lions.

1987: The Howarth Park Bridge was replaced.

1988: September 7, Mayor Bill Moore, conducted the dedication ceremonies for Langus Riverfront Park in honor of Bill Langus, long time councilmember.

Note: Parks such as Alder Street and View Ridge Parks are owned by a Neighborhood Association and maintained by the City. Some parks have been leased to the Department on a '99 Year Lease Agreement such as Doyles Park, which was given to the Department by the School District.

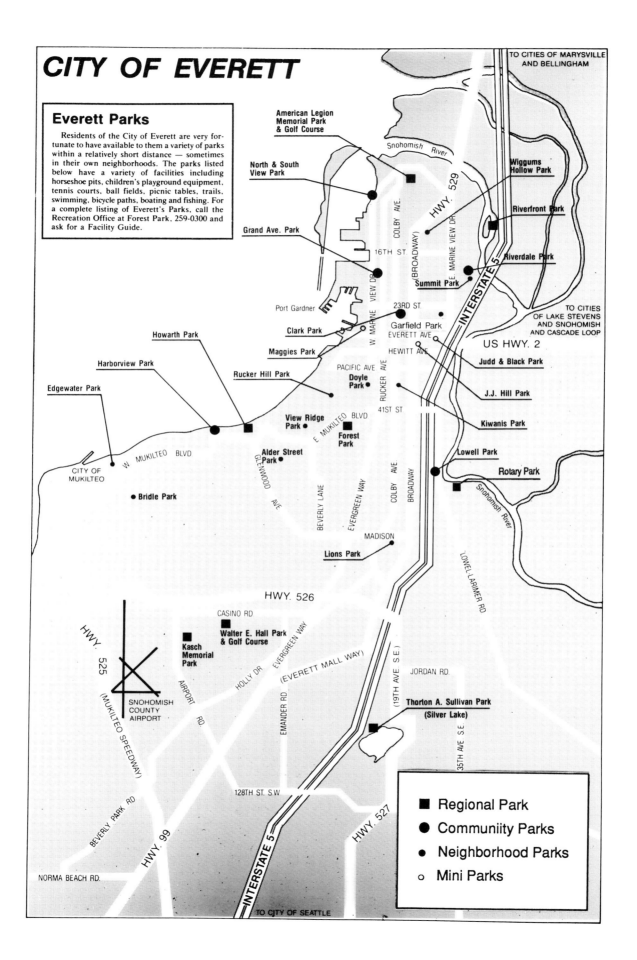

CITY OF EVERETT

Everett Parks

Residents of the City of Everett are very fortunate to have available to them a variety of parks within a relatively short distance — sometimes in their own neighborhoods. The parks listed below have a variety of facilities including horseshoe pits, children's playground equipment, tennis courts, ball fields, picnic tables, trails, swimming, bicycle paths, boating and fishing. For a complete listing of Everett's Parks, call the Recreation Office at Forest Park, 259-0300 and ask for a Facility Guide.

TO CITIES OF MARYSVILLE AND BELLINGHAM

American Legion Memorial Park & Golf Course

North & South View Park

Snohomish River

Wiggums Hollow Park

Riverfront Park

Grand Ave. Park

16TH ST.

COLBY AVE.

HWY. 529

(BROADWAY)

E. MARINE VIEW DR

INTERSTATE 5

Riverdale Park

Summit Park

Port Gardner

23RD ST.

Garfield Park

EVERETT AVE.

TO CITIES OF LAKE STEVENS AND SNOHOMISH AND CASCADE LOOP

Clark Park

HEWITT AVE.

US HWY. 2

Howarth Park

Maggies Park

PACIFIC AVE.

RUCKER AVE.

Judd & Black Park

Harborview Park

Rucker Hill Park

Doyle Park

J.J. Hill Park

Edgewater Park

View Ridge Park

E MUKILTEO BLVD

41ST ST.

Kiwanis Park

W MUKILTEO BLVD

Forest Park

COLBY AVE.

BROADWAY

Lowell Park

Rotary Park

CITY OF MUKILTEO

Alder Street Park

GLENWOOD AVE.

Snohomish River

Bridle Park

BEVERLY LANE

EVERGREEN WAY

LOWELL-LARIMER RD.

MADISON

Lions Park

HWY. 526

CASINO RD

Walter E. Hall Park & Golf Course

EVERGREEN WAY

HWY. 525 (MUKILTEO SPEEDWAY)

Kasch Memorial Park

HOLLY DR

EMANDER RD.

(EVERETT MALL WAY)

(19TH AVE S.E.)

JORDAN RD.

AIRPORT RD.

SNOHOMISH COUNTY AIRPORT

35TH AVE. S.E.

Thorton A. Sullivan Park (Silver Lake)

128TH ST. SW

BEVERLY PARK RD.

HWY. 99

INTERSTATE 5

HWY. 527

NORMA BEACH RD.

TO CITY OF SEATTLE

■ Regional Park

● Communiity Parks

• Neighborhood Parks

○ Mini Parks

Index

About the Authors

Allan May

Allan May was born and reared in Chicago Illinois. He attended the University of Illinois where he earned a bachelor of science degree in journalism. He moved to the Northwest in 1949 after marrying a Snohomish girl. Once in the state, he attended the University of Washington and earned a masters degree in communications.

Compiling over forty years in the field of journalism, Allan May has worked for newspapers from New York to Seattle and has earned several awards for journalism excellence. He has also authored several books including, The *Sea People of Ozette* and *A Voice in the Wilderness.* It was his interest in Snohomish County's history which led him to become involved with this book.

Working as a freelance journalist, Allan May currently resides in Everett's historic Lowell neighborhood with his wife Eleanor and four children, Elizabeth, Martha, Meridith, and Melinda.

Dale Preboski

There was a time, some twenty years ago, when Dale Preboski found Everett a gray place to live. Everett's color was not immediately apparent to this newcomer from the Midwest, but her affection for the place grew and, like many of Everett's early settlers, she chose to stay.

Dale Preboski has been with the *Herald* newspaper for thirteen years. Currently the newspaper's Special Publications Editor, she also serves on the paper's editorial board. As a community volunteer, Dale holds a committee chair in the Everett Sister Cities Association. She is a member of the Everett School District's Curriculum Advisory Board and the board of directors of the Northwest Telco Credit Union.

With daughter, Stefin, and son, Todd, the family was recently joined in marriage to John Hinchcliffe and daughters Christa and Noel. They are at home in a historic section of North Everett.

Ralph Mackey

After graduating from Everett High School in 1949, Ralph Mackey went on to the University of Pudget Sound where he earned a bachelor of arts degree in business, with a minor in history and graduate credits in economics and journalism.

The majority of his years in the work force lie with the Washington Stove Works where he started as a janitor and retired as its CEO.

Mackey's service in the community has been far reaching. He served as Washington State Parks Commissioner for twelve years, a Park Board member for nine years, a Pacific Crest Trail Commission member for seven years, as well as being involved in the National Society for Park Resources, Salvation Army Board, Everett Chamber of Commerce Board, Evergreen Safety Council, Boy Scouts, and Red Cross. Currently he is involved with the Washington State Parks Foundation, Interagency Commission for Outdoor Recreation, Friends of Parks, Mountaineers, and Mountain Rescue.

His accomplishments range from climbing major mountains in North and South America, Africa, Australia, and Asia to earning the Everett City Pride Award from the Everett City Council.